Numb?

Break Old Habits. Escape The Rat Race.
Live Your Ideal Life

*Mr Emerald!
Thank you so much for the gift of TED*. You have made a significant impact in my lives and the lives of all the men I work with. Your work is Truly a gift of creation to this world*

*Be Well
Much Gratitude*

Mar 23/2021

Dave Sinclair

Numb?
Copyright © 2020 Dave Sinclair
Cover Art by Teshia Saunders
Interior Design and Typesetting by Paul Neuviale

All Rights Reserved.

No part of this book may be reproduced or transmitted in any form by any means, electronic or mechanical, including photocopying and recording, or by any information storage and retrieval system, except as may be expressly permitted in writing from the author. The views and opinions expressed in this book are those of the author and do not necessarily belong to any other club, organization, company, or individual.

Book Summary: *Numb?* lays out the four steps to successfully transitioning and changing your life into your ideal future.

Distribution by KDP Amazon and Ingram Spark
P.O.D.
Printed in the United States of America and Canada

Title: Numb?
Names: Dave Sinclair - author

www.davesinclair.ca

ISBN: 978-1-7774076-0-5 (print)
ISBN: 978-1-7774076-1-2 (print workbook)
ISBN: 978-1-7774076-2-9 (e-book)

This book is dedicated to you, the reader. To the searcher in you. It is dedicated to that part of you that wants to connect with what is truly important. I wish you well on your journey, fellow traveler, and I am excited for what you may discover inside of yourself as you read through this book.

To My Readers

My goal behind writing *Numb?* is to help you feel connected again, to what is TRULY important to you. This book is a resource that can help you reconnect to your values and assist you to create and connect to action steps to a life, business, or anything you have only dreamt of before. Think of this book as a launching pad for success.

Within these chapters, you'll notice some extra space where you can take some notes or even doodle which is always a good idea. You'll find the act of writing things down helps to bring your thoughts to life. I suggest using a pencil to allow for easier revisions because, as you go through this process, you might find yourself modifying or building on your answers from previous sections as you progress. Have fun with it.

> If you are not a fan of writing in books, or if you want bigger versions of the worksheets to write in, no problem!
> You can download a companion workbook on my website at
> **www.davesinclair.ca/numbbustingresources**
> or purchase a paperback workbook/journal version on Amazon.

NOTE: The case studies in this book are based on clients that Dave has worked with in the past. While the names have been changed and some of the case studies represent a combination of client experiences they are all representative of the results that have transpired.

Table of Contents

Part One. Taking That First Step Back

1. Are you REALLY Happy? 6
2. One Step Back Beats Two Steps Forward. 21
3. The Power of the Pause. 32
4. Your Ultimate Value Creator 41
5. The Empty Teacup 51
6. The 4 Stages of Stepping Back 55
7. Stage One – Calling Out Change 61
8. Stage Two – Visualizing an Oasis in the Desert 77
9. Stage Three – One Bite at a Time 86
10. Stage Four – Prepare to Enjoy the Marathon 95
11. Step Back in Your Daily Life… Let It Sink In 100
12. Continuously Walking Through the Stages 106

Part Two. Moving Forward by Stepping Back!

13. The Art and Science of Creating Your Ideal Life . . . 123
14. Your Ideal Business. 172
15. Your Ideal Transition. 210
16. A Call to Action 254

Appendix. Further Reading. 257

PART ONE
Taking That First Step Back

HAPPINESS comes from finding meaning and purpose in your life, from the inside.

I know. I chased it from all angles. I thought if I just kept climbing ladders, performing 24/7, as long as I did more, had more, and appeared successful then perhaps I could be happy. Guess what? The happiness I was so desperately chasing, the chase that practically destroyed everything in my path, was right there all the time. I just never noticed. I was too busy being busy.

I was a partner in a multinational company that was in ever-increasing growth. I did more than well enough but never felt truly happy. Stuck in the rat race of working long hours to meet projections and earn my living I could not see what it was I was missing out on. I created a false sense of purpose for myself that consumed my time, and was reinforced by financial rewards. I used the money the role provided to chase happiness, keeping my whole identity wrapped up in the work I did but ironically, I was never able to be happy because I lacked identity and purpose outside of the business. I lacked a connection to what would truly make me happy, and I lacked a method to help me re-discover this connection.

If I wanted to get out of it I would have to dig deeper and find a more well-rounded sense of identity, but back then I was not able to do the necessary work to transform my life. So I stayed numb.

By the fall of 2011, I grew even more frustrated with the business. I was tired of the chase while never feeling satisfied, so I decided that if I couldn't fix my relationship with the business, I would have to leave. I would have to look for happiness elsewhere.

I had no real plan; I just knew something had to change.

In spite of the unknowns, I left in 2012. I just couldn't do it anymore. I knew that money wasn't making me happy. I knew that my identity as a business owner wasn't making me happy. I knew that the perks of a high ranking position didn't make me happy. So, what was I there for if none of it was making me happy? The exit was successful from a financial point of view. I was bought out and was no longer a part of the business. On the first day after I left, my email was no longer functioning. There was nothing coming into my inbox. And there it was, I WASN'T NEEDED!

The stress of working in corporate was gone and I was left with something more fundamental to consider: *Now, if I'm not a business owner, who am I?* I was thrown head-first into a massive existential crisis. If you can imagine a train at full speed piling into a solid concrete wall, well, you get the picture.

What would become of me now? Yup. I was in a pickle.

I found myself quite lost those first few months and actually started filling my time with drinking and feeling sorry for myself. I finally had the freedom I sought but no idea what to do and no idea where to start.

Emotionally numbed out, even though I looked fine on the outside, I couldn't understand what was going on with me. This got in the way of my ability to take charge of situations that were problematic to the point where I wasn't able to confront, process or manage my emotions. I just kept looking for happiness everywhere but inside.

Grinding it out in the trenches and hustling for the hope of happiness in the future often makes you miserable in the present. Plus, will that future ever become a reality? Or will you always be chasing it? When believing that happiness comes from staying in step with society's expectations or hustling for a better future stops working for you, what then?

Famous psychologist Viktor Frankl said that "It is the very pursuit of happiness that thwarts happiness."

When we're looking everywhere for that something that will finally make us happy, we're not present with what is here for us now. We pretend we're good but meanwhile, we're busying ourselves with new purchases, lavish vacations, getting lost in drinking and partying and there is limited joy to be found in these external distractions.

> "Happiness cannot be pursued; it must ensue.
> One must have a reason to be happy."
>
> VIKTOR FRANKL

A recent study by Dr. Todd Kashdan (Professor of Psychology, George Mason University) actually proved Viktor Frankl right by showing that the greater emphasis its participants put on happiness, the less happy they were. In the study, Dr. Kashdan found that people who put the greatest emphasis on being happy reported 50 percent less frequent positive emotions, 35 percent less satisfaction about their life, and 75 percent with more depressive symptoms.

So, how do we stop the chase, become happy, and start living our ideal life?

The crux of the issue comes down to happiness and meaning.

Happiness and meaning are different, and happiness without meaning really doesn't lead to a great life.

But… chasing happiness, numbing ourselves, and feeling that everything is not fine is quite common in the business world. It's at the root of how I now help business owners and other people today. I help them find meaning and purpose and then use this to get them a plan in place. The result is regaining control of their life.

It wasn't until I had hit rock bottom by landing in a cell that I realized something had to change. My journey of a thousand steps began when I finally understood that the something that had to change was me.

≈

I share this story with you because I want you to know you are not alone. Chasing happiness and feeling numb is more common than you think. But you can live your ideal life and feel happy. I know because I woke up, took back my life, stopped feeling numb, and started living my ideal life. It didn't happen overnight. It took work. But it was all worth it. I believe you can take those first steps toward your ideal life just like I did.

Things can change, you can change, and this book will help you find your way.

CHAPTER 1
Are you REALLY Happy?

I woke up cold and alone. I was lying on a hard bunk with a stainless steel toilet beside me. Looking around, I saw that I was locked up in a windowless room without access to anyone else. What the hell was going on? I was in a detention cell. How did I end up here? What happened? And then it all started to flood back to me: The previous night. The partying. Blacking out drunk. Being too loud and carrying on. Taking exception to the police who showed up. Party Dave had come out to play again.

As if landing in a cold hard cell wasn't bad enough, this happened while we were out of town for a hockey tournament with my son. These away tournaments were always a great time with family and friends and there was almost always a couple of late nights that involved some drinking for the parents. But, as with many people with addictions, I thought everyone was as drunk as I was. I wasn't aware that I was using family and leisure time to escape my misery but being locked in a cell woke me up to see that things were not going well for me.

So there you have it. My rock bottom.

Why do I share this now, and why with you?

This story I share with you has nothing to do with wanting your pity, understanding, empathy or anything else. I'm writing to tell you that the stakes are high and your ability to have a business and life you love can easily elude you. So if you are in a situation that feels anything like the one I was in I want to know: Do you want to stay there? Do you want to stay numb to it all? What will it take for you to wake up and realize things need to change?

Perhaps you aren't yet at rock bottom, but what is your life, your business, and your career telling you right now? Are you feeling numb or lacking purpose and direction? Are you searching for something different?

Is it more time with family?

Is it better life satisfaction?

Is it finding deeper meaning and purpose?

Do you want more freedom from your business?

What questions led you to pick up this book?

What circumstances led you to these questions?

You can reach out, get off the rat race, and start working toward living your ideal life at any moment. You don't have to wait to hit rock bottom for your new journey to begin.

THE BACK STORY

I didn't just wake up in a cell one day. There were plenty of earlier indicators that I could have paid attention to but I ignored them all. Numbing out does that. It took hitting rock bottom to wake me up.

These indicators were warnings, like "check engine" lights. What they were really trying to tell me was not so much about external situations but significant internal shifts that were needed if I wanted to head toward what really mattered to me in both my business and life.

Back in 2010, before I had found myself in a detention cell, I had the life. Everything money could buy. My head got big, after all I was partner in a big company so I believed I was a Very Important Person. Work took over my life and left me with a mountain of worries, unrelenting demands on my time, many sleepless nights and my personal relationships in ruins. The harder I worked to gain the happiness I sought, the more I numbed, and the more I got lost in the work. I gave so much of myself to my career that everything else suffered. Can you relate? It's so easy for this to happen.

From the outside looking in, I had the life people envied; partner in a company, lots of money, beautiful home, lavish vacations; I could afford anything I wanted. On the flip side; I was stressed out, 60 lbs. overweight, drank way too much, and my family life suffered. All of this was not good for my family or for me. But what to do? How to change? I was in this rat race that had no finish line.

When you are in the rat race, there's nobody waiting at the end to give you a medal and dump a cooler of Gatorade over your head. The wheel just keeps spinning. And the longer you're caught in this cycle of consumption, the more natural it becomes. It becomes a habit that is hard to escape from. You end up forgetting that you are not living that ideal life and become numb instead.

I remember thinking there had to be more to life than this and I spent a lot of time I didn't have wondering, **"Is this all there is? What else is out there for me?"**

One day, as I sat in my office at the end of a typically long and stressful day I poured myself a stiff drink and like a video playing I watched my future unfold. I saw myself continuing on this path and leading myself not to the happiness I chased, but to an early grave. My original purpose and calling were lost in the past and my future looked like a disaster. I might die of a heart attack sitting at my desk. What was I doing this for and at what cost?

When did it all turn into me running in a hamster wheel to get more, more, more? I kept trying to fill the emptiness inside with more lavish vacations, buying better cars and a nicer home but I felt even more hollow and unhappy.

When I first entered the workforce and started making more and more money it all felt so good. I needed a nice car to take important clients around town in, and a big house to demonstrate my success. But these things I accumulated didn't do anything to improve my quality of life. In fact, the more money I made, the more stuff I needed. When you live for the rat race you can never actually get ahead because your burn rate keeps pace with what you make. So even if you get that promotion, are you actually happy or are you just burned out?

This was a key warning and it came to me many years before I found myself in that cell. Buying and doing more to manufacture happiness may work in the short term (like while you're on vacation), but the feeling quickly fades once you return to the hamster wheel.

Trying to buy happiness may be a good indicator you have some internal work ahead!

So, originally I thought it was my work that was causing all my stress. The work, the job, and outside interference had to be the reason my life felt like it was falling apart.

I looked at how I could shift my role in the business. Could others do my job? Probably. But I didn't want to ever admit it. So instead of letting others take on some of my workload, I held on to every task because I couldn't trust anyone else. I mean, who could possibly be as good as me?

This was another key warning. I had fooled myself into thinking I was indispensable, and the business needed me to survive.

I believed I was more important than I actually was. As business owners and partners we constantly think no one can do as good of a job as us. We have this god-like complex. But it is false. If we trained the right person, they could start taking on the tasks we don't like. Giving us more time to be the boss and lead the company into the right direction and creating new growth.

Being indispensable isn't a reality, though. I arranged it so the business would need me. I needed it to need me.

The feeling of wanting to be indispensable is, in fact, quite common in the business world, and it's at the root of how I help business owners, managers, and others today. I help people find real meaning and purpose they can use to build their life and business on. The result is a foundation for their ideal life and ideal business.

Looking back at my own situation, I can clearly see I lacked identity and purpose outside of the business. My lack of identity and values is what cultivated my need to be in control and to feel indispensable. Back then, all I had was the business. I didn't have anything else in my life. At least that is what I thought at the time. So if I wasn't in the business, who was I? If someone could perform my role as well or even better, where did that leave me? Talk about having insecurities! I created a false sense of purpose for myself that consumed my time so I would not be able to seek what I really wanted. Or that is what I told myself. But what this false identity or purpose really did was protect me from the fact that I had lost touch with what I valued. I once had values, but they got lost in time and didn't grow with me. My original values never wanted to join the rat race.

By the fall of 2011, I became even more frustrated with the business or maybe it was myself. I just knew that I had to get out of it and that I wanted to feel stress-free. So, I left and with it, I also left behind my entire sense of self. All that I identified with stayed behind.

As mentioned previously, the exit was a financially sound one. In the first few months I was feeling lost and sorry for myself. I filled my time with drinking. I finally had the freedom I wanted but no idea what to do and no idea where to start. I had time, but no hobbies, and no idea how to build a life that gave me happiness.

Unfortunately, it took a night in a jail cell to wake me up. It made me realize something had to change and that something had to be me.

Being in that cell kickstarted my first step toward finding my ideal life.

You can have everything you say you want… when you adapt and change. This book will help you find your way.

What is it in your story that led you toward this book, and how might you want to change that story?

Perhaps you are unhappy with your business, perhaps you are living an unhealthy life. Maybe you want to connect more with friends and family or seek more fulfillment. Perhaps you want to go from feeling numb to simply feeling alive.

Whatever you're looking for, it starts with admitting you want change. It is about saying you are ready to leave behind the past and start your journey toward the future.

I want to encourage you to step back and see that the time for change is always right in front of you. It's a choice and only you can make it.

MY FIRST STEPS

When I woke up in the jail cell that morning on March 10, 2012, I thought about what I hadn't yet accomplished and what I could do. I asked myself about the final story in my life. What did I want it to be about? Until then, I would have predicted my gravestone would read, "RIP. Dave died young, was a great worker, and had lots of nice stuff."

What will yours read? Imagine for a moment you are at your own funeral, watching it from above. What is it you want people to say about your life?

A few weeks after that night in the cell, I read my first book in a very long time, *Man's Search for Meaning* by Viktor Frankl. Reading that book inspired my journey and influenced the rest of my life. It made me think about how I want to live my life, what I actually want people to say about me right now and at my funeral. It also led me to taking a step back by checking into a treatment center.

Viktor Frankl survived as a World War II prisoner in the concentration camps of Nazi Germany. Not only did he survive, but his experience helped him see the truth of Nietzsche's statement that "[he] who has a 'why' to live for can bear with almost any how."

In short, he believed that unhappiness derives from a lack of meaning. Through his life, he found that when people were able to uncover meaning in their lives, they were much better able to find happiness and flourish. Chasing happiness as an end in itself can lead us to be overly focused and stressed. Instead, he believed finding meaning in our lives in our activities and experiences—leads to happiness.

According to Frankl, we can find meaning in three main ways:

1. We can find meaning in the work we do and the things we accomplish
2. We can find meaning in experiences, such as discovering the beauty in nature, appreciating art, loving others, etc.
3. We can find meaning in suffering that cannot be prevented by shifting our perspective.

"Everything can be taken from a man but one thing: the last of human freedoms — to choose one's attitude in any given set of circumstances, to choose one's own way," Frankl wrote.

How does this translate to life?

We must get in touch with what is important to us and then work toward setting goals, doing things, and having experiences that in and of themselves feel important and purposeful. By doing this, we'll discover happiness and a deeper sense of meaning.

In short, you'll feel like you have more meaning and purpose when you live in a way and do things that you value. Living in alignment with your values lies at the heart of this book, and I urge you to keep this concept in mind as you move through your journey.

To illustrate how meaning can flow from suffering, I offer my own example. In those early days after winding up in the cell, I could have chosen many ways to go. Believe me, I sat in self-pity for a while but it shook me up and soon I started moving forward. I decided to start the work I needed to do on myself to remove the source of much of my suffering. This was step one.

The next step related to how I choose to deal with what I could not change: I shifted my perspective from feeling sorry for myself about what had led me to that cell to embracing the past for teaching me what did not fit in my life anymore. Ultimately these lessons helped me learn and grow to the point that now I am able to help others find their own path to meaning and purpose.

As you read this, can you think back to mistakes you've made or experiences that were less than ideal? If these events are still hard to deal with, is there any way you may be able to hold onto them a little less tightly and perhaps even find some meaning in what you learned from them?

The path I chose is allowing me to become who I am today. It has led me to uncovering my mission to help individuals and organizations discover their own definition of success – one that is well rounded and rooted in values and then empower them to get there.

The feeling you get from pursuing your ideal version of success and life is that of meaning and purpose. As a coach, I work with people who feel like they are sleepwalking through life. They wonder where things went wrong and lack the passion to find those first steps to move forward. I also used to walk through life without meaning. But I got out and worked my way toward having what I describe as my ideal life.

My work with clients has ranged from helping startup entrepreneurs figure out if getting into business is right for them, working with companies to adopt a strategic planning mindset, and coaching large family businesses through succession. In addition, I have worked with individuals recovering from various states of addiction, as well as coached people to discover and move toward the next phase of their journey.

There is no one-size-fits-all equation to finding your ideal life and ideal version of success. It all starts with defining what is most important in any given situation. Once you tap into this process, life and business will take on more meaning. It will give you hope and a path to your ideal future. Tap into this and add a plan and the passion to take a small step everyday. Who knows how far you can go!

Now, let's fast forward from that jail cell to the present day. Currently, I'm very healthy, I don't drink, I run full marathons, I'm more in love with my wife than ever before, I have a rich and meaningful spiritual connection to this world, I treasure relationships in my life, and I do what I feel is very meaningful work.

I went from the lowest of lows to enjoying life. Don't get me wrong, each day is still a stepping-stone to the future, but I know that both the journey and the destination can be more fulfilling.

You can do this, too. You can find your answers to your questions and start taking action now!

And really that is the purpose of this book. The book is a guide to help you figure out:

- Do you want more out of life?
- Do you want more out of your business?
- Do you want a transition plan that works for you?

Not only will this book help you kickstart the process of finding your answers, it will also help you do this in a way that can allow you to more thoroughly enjoy your journey.

Why these three areas?

- For many business owners, they are interconnected.
- Once you figure out what you want in life, the other pieces—your business and transition—more easily fall into place.

Your ideal life, business and transition are like separate legs on a three-legged stool. You need them all to properly support you.

You can't have your ideal life if you don't take the time to step back and answer what it is that you want. Once you can see and feel what you want in your life, you can look at where you are right now, and start taking action to move forward.

Having an idea of what your ideal life looks like can help you set a vision and steer your business toward goals that align with your ideal life. You can turn your attention to it with newfound passion and purpose and transform it so you can start living truer to your ideal life. To get there, you'll need a plan that will turn the business into that ideal vision.

As you start to progress down the path toward your ideal life and ideal business, you can ask the same things of your ideal transition. You'll begin to see how your entire identity is not tied up in the business. And as your business moves closer and closer to its ideal state, it may require you less and less, which in turn gives you more transition options and a clearer future.

That's right. Once you take the time to step back and figure out what it is you want out of life, the rest of the work starts to fall into place much easier.

Are you ready to be happy?

There's a better way to live. A path that can take you from feeling numb to fully alive. A path to your own unique meaning and purpose. And, unlike me, you don't have to hit rock bottom to begin.

HOW MIGHT THIS BOOK HELP YOU?

Using the tools in this book, I got my train back on the tracks. Now I am sharing everything I learned with you!

The most important new habit I developed that helped me start getting my life on track was stepping back. I could not have made the changes had I not learned the power of *stepping back*, taking a pause, and asking the deep questions that allowed me to see just how right my life could be.

You can find your own definition of success and make it a reality, too. I'll help you make sense of where you are, where you want to go, and how you will get there. I'll give you a plan to increase your odds of a successful and less stressful journey. And I hope I'll help you feel less alone along the way.

A key to this is that I'll ask you to take a more balanced approach and look at the entire system of your life. What do you really want your life to look and feel like? This means not just in terms of work but also in terms of family, health, spirituality, and whatever other aspect of your life you value. I'll help you to not only uncover your own definition of success but also help you make it a reality.

For business owners, in particular, I strongly believe the key creator of value in a business is an owner who is fully in touch with the sense of purpose provided by their business and how it fits into their vision of an ideal life.

So, STEP BACK. Let's see what's been missing from your present and what is possible for your future. Let's stop chasing happy and start getting still so we can start living our lives passionately, purposefully, and eradicate the numb.

• STEP BACK REFLECTION •

Do you have any early warning lights blinking at you on your dashboard of life?

_____
_____
_____
_____
_____
_____
_____
_____
_____
_____

On a scale of 1-10 with 1 being: I am totally dissatisfied with my life, and 10 being: Life could not get any better, where do you rank your life, and what thoughts do you have about what is making it this way?

_____
_____
_____
_____
_____
_____
_____
_____
_____
_____

• STEP BACK REFLECTION •

What might be a few things, that if worked at, could lead to a deeper feeling of fulfillment, and happiness in your life?

_____
_____
_____
_____
_____
_____
_____
_____
_____
_____

What do you want the people closest to you to say about how you lived your life?

_____
_____
_____
_____
_____
_____
_____
_____
_____
_____

CHAPTER 2
One Step Back Beats Two Steps Forward

You will likely find it odd to talk of stepping back when you've been programmed to just keep moving forward. But it's not.

To take a step back is to take time and give yourself the permission to better understand your "why." It's when you briefly hit the "pause" button and think about what your goals and values are. Often triggered by a significant change, the step back allows you to better see what may need to shift (both externally and internally) to ensure you can gently and more gracefully step into the change.

The step back process is about giving yourself the space to become mindful so you can tap into who you are and what you want, where you are and where you want to go and finally; what it's going to take for you to get there.

Being mindful (or using mindfulness) is a superpower you can develop and it will help you go from living on autopilot to taking control of your life and business. The practical methods set out in this book will help you do just that.

Stop, take a deep breath in, hold it for a few seconds, slowly release it, and then pause again before your next inhale. Repeat this a couple more times. Now allow your breathing to return to normal. Taking a step back could be as simple as catching yourself before reacting and breathing mindfully for even just a minute.

I invite you to pause and take a few moments to think about what you want to achieve with this book. What reason did you envision or think of? With this reason in mind, what do you notice going on inside of you? What emotions come up for you as you think about what you want?

After a minute or so, take another deep breath in through your nose and then fully breathe out through your mouth. To me, this is a simple mindfulness technique that you can use anytime, anywhere. It's a tool that can help you not only set your path forward but do it in a way that connects you to what you value.

There is no right way or wrong way to progress through this book, and any of the following ways could work:

- Take a camping trip by yourself for a few days and don't bring your cell phone. Just this book and a notebook.
- Check into a hotel for a day by yourself.
- Find a regular time each day to sit by yourself and go through the steps.
- After a significant change in your life or business, take some time off to relax and refresh by going through this process.
- Go on a vacation with your family and mark some time off each day to think of these questions. Perhaps do it first thing in the morning on the beach before anyone wakes up.

- Or, just find a few moments here and there, and start with that. It can be as simple as waking up 15 minutes earlier and using that time to work through this book or stopping by a café once a week.

The key point is for you to make a bit of time where you can be by yourself and sink into the process. Find what works for you and your situation.

> **• BONUS THOUGHT •**
>
> Imagine you did build a simple habit like putting some time aside every day to work on this book. If you keep this habit up and it became second nature, what might you tackle next with this time? What new habit would you want to take on? Each small habit you take on might seem small, but it adds up over time and can create massive success and happiness within your life and business.

Creating a little space in your life so you can step back to answer a few really big questions can kickstart anything! Have you ever heard the phrase, "You can't take care of anyone else until you have properly taken care of yourself?" That's the step back.

❧

Before we go on, I invite you to imagine a scenario.

Think about a spot you really enjoy. A spot that brings you great joy and fulfillment. Now I invite you to imagine you are there right now. Take a few deep breaths in and out. As you breathe allow yourself to feel what it is to be fully in this spot right now.

What is it like to be there?

What do you notice?

How do you feel right now?

Take a moment here and really enjoy this time.

What would you invest to start progressing down a path of more fulfillment in your life, your business, and your career that would allow you to tap into the feeling of being in that perfect spot even more? What if all you had to do was invest a little time?

WHAT CAME UP FOR YOU AS YOU SAT WITH THIS IDEA?

Perhaps your thoughts of change have been jolted into place because of a health scare, or a divorce, or the failure of a business, to name a few possible scenarios. Perhaps a significant event hasn't happened, but you think it's time to make it happen. What might need to shift internally so you can prepare to step into the change process, move through the muddiness that you will likely encounter in the change, and then more fully step into the change you envision?

Although this book does not explicitly discuss the psychology of change, it's important to address the shifts that are necessary for change to occur.

Consider this example:

> *Imagine for a moment someone who has a business. The business is doing well financially, but this person must be there all the time and has very little time to be at home. He decides a change is needed.*
>
> *He envisions a new business where great people are in place helping with the work and freeing up his time.*
>
> *Great right?*
>
> *Now, imagine a coaching conversation around this situation.*
>
> *Coach: What might be holding you back from hiring the support staff you know would help?*
>
> *Business owner: There aren't any qualified people out there that can do as good a job as I do quoting and dealing with customers.*
>
> *Coach: If this were not the case, and great people were available, what might this allow you to do?*

Business owner: Well, I guess it would allow me to focus on other things and have a bit more time.

Coach: What would you do tomorrow if you did have more time?

Business owner: I would spend it with my family.

Coach: What about spending more time with family appeals to you?

The business owner explains how much he loves his family and how they would also be able to do a few more things, like go for a walk, read some books, etc.

Coach: I noticed some concern come over your face as you talked about the things you seem you want to do, but I have a sense something else may be holding you back. Do you have any insights on what this may be?

Business owner: I've been away from my family emotionally for so long that I fear they may not want to have me around.

Coach: I am curious what you feel might need to shift inside of you to allow you to move beyond this fear?

Business owner: I'm not sure, but perhaps I may need to gain the feeling that my family would be willing to have me around a bit more. Perhaps this would allow me to better see that there can be more to this life than work. I think perhaps I have been allowing my work to need me as an excuse so I don't have to deal with my fear of not being loved by my family.

Sometimes we want external changes, but those require us to make internal changes, too. The business owner had the resources to hire the people that would allow him to have more time, which was the external shift, but his internal state held him back from making this change.

In this case, before he even attempts the external shift, he may need to spend some time addressing the internal shift. Perhaps he has a conversation with his family or goes through some additional coaching before he hires more people. Perhaps there are more internal shifts he needs to make. Are you starting to get an idea of any internal shifts you may want to make?

Without the internal shift, the external shift will likely fail or at the least, be very hard to sustain.

I wish I had understood this all a little more before I stepped away from my business.

These internal shifts can be a bit complex and can take time. There is seldom a straight line from where you are to where you want to be. As we start to make changes, we will often encounter discomforts inside us we didn't know were there.

It does not always have to be this complex, but once you decide to make a change, it can often lead you down a winding path. One discovery, and a few steps forward, may lead you to more insights, and doing work somewhere else. The problem comes in when you have no plan, or any awareness of what change might ensue.

These smaller steps and the process through them can be a bit muddy. William Bridges, the author of the book *Transitions: Making Sense of Life's Changes*, called this muddiness the "neutral zone."

The neutral zone is a period after something ends and before something else begins. Think of it like this: When I decided to leave my old business as its partner, it was an end. That end sent me to a transition zone. What I can see now is that I needed to press pause here after the end. I should have taken a bit more time, to allow things to process a bit more. Processing the ending would have served me and would have given me more time to think about what I wanted.

You see, it is here in the transition zone that you can find yourself, your true self, and let go of things you may need to let go of before you move on to a new beginning. Unfortunately, for many of us we're very uncomfortable sitting still for a while doing this work as we think we are "doing nothing". So instead of sitting still we busy ourselves to either avoid the neutral zone, and its discomfort, or we forget to take a moment to honor the transitions between major life events, significant projects, or other changes no matter how big or small.

All change is significant and can benefit from moving properly through the transition process.

The transition process has three stages:

1. Ending, Losing, and Letting Go.

When something ends or is about to end, it is important to allow it the time and space to honor what was. Skipping past this step can keep us stuck and ruminating on the past worrying and wondering.

2. The Neutral Zone.

The neutral zone is where we can further allow ourselves the proper time to grieve, further let go of limitations that may be holding us back, start looking inward toward what it is we really want, create empowering beliefs, get in touch with our values, and create a vision for a new beginning.

3. The New Beginning.

If we take the time to do the first two steps we can then step into our new beginning with a plan, and a sense of passion. These items will help to make it happen which will increase our chances of success!

Stepping back is beneficial at every point in the transition process to see what may need attention and to set new direction.

Life does not include a GPS that takes you directly from point A to point B, so stepping back helps set the general direction and acts as a compass to ensure you are still going in the right general direction. That said, I don't believe there is ever a straight path forward and often some of our best insights come from some wrong turns. Having a bit of a plan and process can help. I know it helps me now and have seen it help many people with whom I have worked.

• STEP BACK REFLECTION •

Press pause for a moment, take a deep breath and then answer the below questions

What would be valuable for you to accomplish while reading this book?

_____
_____
_____
_____
_____
_____
_____
_____
_____

Are any external or internal shifts coming to mind that may benefit from some exploration?

_____
_____
_____
_____
_____
_____
_____
_____
_____

• STEP BACK REFLECTION •

If you are looking at a significant change in your life or business, is there something that may end for you? If so how might you honor that part to allow you to better prepare for the change ahead?

CHAPTER 3
The Power of the Pause

When I left my business and ultimately landed in that jail cell, I had no clue what I wanted from my life. I was 40 years old and all I knew was that something vital was missing. I was determined to discover what it was. Of course that something vital was ME, but I didn't know that, yet.

Stepping back and taking a pause at that point was the most profound thing I could have done.

I checked myself into a 30-day addictions recovery program that focused on renewed meaning and purpose. This may not be for everyone, but for me, it was the kickstart I needed. Taking this pause allowed me to discover how deeply I yearned to take the inner journey that would lead me to a happier life.

But I was still stuck. I didn't know how to look at my faults without beating myself up for not being perfect. I had been brought up to be strong, and independent, not just at home, but also in my career and business life. Men were not supposed to have weaknesses, and if we did, we were taught in business to "Fake it till you make it." I thought being vulnerable to the fact that I did not have all the answers showed weakness. What a load of BS.

I didn't know how to be authentic about all of my feelings without seeing myself as weak. I wore a mask of "having it all together." I surrounded myself with more and more shiny things because I didn't know who I was at my core. I was using materialism to mask a false identity.

I didn't understand, yet, that the whole point of life is to tackle your own truth with as much heart as possible, and that becoming who you really are is a lifelong journey. I was chasing happiness through instant gratification and materialism. I had no idea that learning and growing along the way could be so fulfilling.

Then there was a switch. New learnings came in. I sought to welcome more in my life. I started to appreciate the power of reading for the first time in my life. I was hungry for inspiration and guidance, and to know that I wasn't alone. I found a tremendous amount of information then and continue to find gems in almost every book I read.

I learned to meditate. In fact, to this day I find a great deal of solace in having a quiet space to reflect on my journey every morning. Meditation has the power to help us be more relaxed and aware in our day to day interactions. It is a gift to ourselves, and if I was making one suggestion to you here it would be to find a few minutes every day to find a quiet space, bring your attention to your breath and simply be still.

The biggest benefit is that constant practice allows you to become more mindful of everything going on. When you are mindful, you are able to take a second to step back and are then better equipped to respond rather than react to whatever comes up.

I discovered that the empty holes many of us have inside will continue to fill up with stuff we don't want if we ignore them. I acquired some important tools that helped me heal those holes, some were first developed as far back as my childhood.

For instance, I had trouble making friends when I was very young, so I created a defense mechanism. Sometimes I still hear it, a little voice in my head telling me things like, "You don't need friends. You made it this far, haven't you?" Being aware of this experience allows me to tell that little voice to bugger off and put the effort into connecting more with others. Awareness is key.

After my journey was well underway, I learned something else that had an even bigger impact. I learned wanting it ALL is not the problem. The problem is, what IS your all? What is it that you really want out of your life, and what is it that life wants out of you? Realizing this was a game changer in my journey toward my ideal life.

At the end of the day, what do you want your life to have meant, and how do you hope you showed up in your day-to-day interactions? If we can't say what it is we want, how can we expect to be truly happy?

I believe this is why so many of us overdo it with food, alcohol, work, spending money… you name it. We're disconnected from our core sense of self and we're numbing out so we don't have to deal with the hard personal work of discovering what will ultimately lead us to the 'happy' we've been chasing.

It's easy to make excuses. I would never have gotten where I am now if I had not first committed to pausing without any excuses. It doesn't mean you have to completely put things on hold. Actually, it's as simple as finding a quiet spot to sit for 5 minutes a day to pause and find your own answers.

We owe it to ourselves to press pause and connect to what we really want.

This was not the only lesson life had in store for me during my pause.

I'll never forget a conversation I had with a therapist during my initial step back about some beliefs I still held about my past that continued to hold me back. She had enough of my feeling sorry for myself and shook me back to the present.

"Dave, you're just not that f***ing unique," she said.

In other words, she was telling me not to be so hard on myself. We all have baggage; we all have issues. You are not the only person suffering. You are not the only person with a past. You are not the only person who has challenges ahead! She held my hand to let me know I was not alone but also kicked me out of my victim's mindset.

Have you ever felt as if you are the only one suffering or that your struggles are worse than anyone else's? Has that ever held you back from making a change in your life?

Talk about a wake-up call. I laugh about it now, but at the time it shocked me into the realization that I could continue making excuses for myself, or I could accept the fact that we are all dealing with challenges and it was up to me to deal with mine. It was up to me to figure out what I wanted out of life and to move forward.

Of all the moments in my life, I would say this one was the massive catalyst that pushed me ahead. The words still resonate in my mind to this day. Does knowing you're not alone bring you some comfort, too?

The power of the pause to the rescue again!

When we find ourselves dwelling on the past or overthinking issues in the present, what if we look for the hidden lessons and insights these things can provide us? If there is pain or discomfort, thank it for showing us what we don't want in our lives. Once we have a better idea of what we do not want, why not ask ourselves what we really do want?

Being in control of how we view our past and our current challenges means we can dwell in the pain or flourish in the learning it provides us. Seen in this way, our challenges can be a gift, rather than a burden.

I'm excited to work with you on the power of the pause and help you kickstart your journey toward a life of meaning and purpose. You are not alone. Everyone has troubles. If you feel troubled and are wondering what this is all about, your path forward will be custom fit to your own personal definition of success.

Consider how my client Ellie benefited from the power of the pause.

CASE STUDY | MEET ELLIE

Ellie was a single mom and she was in a career in which she felt under utilized. She came to a point where she was feeling stuck, numb; she was just running in circles with nothing growing or changing in her life and her career. She felt that life lacked meaning. She was bored and knew there had to be more to life. She knew that she wanted more, but had no idea where to start.

Taking a step back and looking at her life, her family, and where she currently was, was the first stage we worked on together. It was after she took a step back when she realized she not only wanted more but it was also possible to reach all of her goals. This was the start of developing her growth mindset.

At this point, the next question I asked Ellie was: 'If you could just sit back for a moment and imagine what life could be like for you, what image comes up?'

Ellie said that she dreamed of owning a beautiful European-style café in the mountains where she would serve healthy homemade coffees and treats, provide a place for the community to meet and a space to coach her own clients.

Every time we talked about this vision of hers, Ellie filled with excitement, however, it was obvious that there were some things holding her back. Over time, Ellie was able to see the other parts of her life that were important to her and to understand how they may be affected by owning a café.

Ellie now knows what she wants, she has a vision of her future. But now we need to take another step back and see what it takes to get there.

To get to her ideal life Ellie would have to take some small actionable steps. One of her steps was to evaluate different aspects of her life such as family time, self-care and to take small actions that would move her toward alignment with her vision of her ideal life.

As the coaching sessions progressed, Ellie was taking action to move her career and life into alignment with what she wanted, but along the way she'd be met with more roadblocks and inner gremlins. Negative thinking tried to sabotage her from reaching her ideal life:

How will I ever make this all happen?

What if I am not good enough?

I have never done this before, what makes me think I can do this now?

So many questions popped up for Ellie and the biggest ones were the internal questions that kept shaking her confidence.

One by one, we explored the roadblocks. It took time and effort by Ellie, but she knew it was worth it.

At one point in our coaching, Ellie had found the perfect opportunity to have her café. She was excited to have found the perfect location for the café and was finalizing the startup funding and lease details. She was feeling confident and excited for the future. But as life would have it, Ellie had to walk away from this deal.

Others would have taken this as a complete defeat. Given up on their dream. But not Ellie. She took another pause to reflect and this time she realized how much she had learned and grown. With some more coaching, she tweaked her vision to something that fit her even better.

The new idea and dream tapped into her skills, talents, and added everything she learned in her experiences to give her the confidence and drive to really kickstart her coaching business.

Now she successfully helps her clients through similar experiences as her own.

In less than a year, Ellie had gone from what was only a fleeting dream to a transformation where she now has a plan and is taking the steps needed to reach her ideal business and ideal life.

The process in this book will allow you to take your own step back. It will allow you to harness the power of the pause to help you first set your direction, and as you encounter obstacles along the way, the process will help you tweak your vision as you learn and grow. I am excited for where stepping back can take you!

• STEP BACK REFLECTION •

In what ways might pressing pause more often in your life help you, and as a result, others around you?

_____
_____
_____
_____
_____
_____
_____
_____
_____
_____
_____

In the past, have you felt alone in the challenges you face? What does knowing others face similar challenges do for you mindset?

_____
_____
_____
_____
_____
_____
_____
_____
_____
_____

CHAPTER 4
Your Ultimate Value Creator

When I am working with business owners, an early question that often stumps them is:

What do you want for your life outside the business?

As business owners, we tend to become hyper-focused on the business and oftentimes we lose sight of what we are working for. In fact, it is very common for people to start businesses without a well-rounded vision for what it will take to be successful, and how this may impact their overall life. Often there is too much emphasis on immediate lifestyle upgrades, such as: I will make more money and buy nice things; I will be my own boss and have no one to answer to; I will travel more; I will make my own hours and have more freedom.

YES. These are all wonderful things, but even if you have all that you set out to get for yourself, what do you *really* want? What feelings are you trying to create? And *how* will you get there?

Get really clear on what you ACTUALLY want. Why? Because a very important element of owning a successful business is ensuring it is in alignment with what you want for your life. Evaluating and envisioning your business must come with you evaluating and envisioning other aspects of your life as well. So you can be happy.

Taking the time to step back and define what it is you really want out of life helps give you a target. Without it, you can easily get lost pursuing more money, more work, more whatever in the business until the day comes that you realize that *it* is running you rather than you running it.

Many of my clients are tired. They're stressed. They spend all of their time working hard in the business, rarely finding the time to work on the business. When pressed about why they want to work on the business, many say, "So I can have more time to focus on my life."

What are some of the reasons business owners say they can't find time?

Well, I can't find the right people.

No one can do what I do, the way I do.

I don't have time to train people.

I just can't trust anyone to do this work.

I don't know how to delegate so I have to do everything myself.

I don't have the money for that.

I'm in over my head and can't climb out.

So we end up doing everything ourselves and feeling overwhelmed. This is a trap that often holds our business back as much as it holds us back from living our ideal life.

CASE STUDY | MEET PAUL

Paul is a successful business owner with over 80 employees. He began working with me because he was feeling overwhelmed and could not find any free time for himself. He felt stuck in the day to day aspects of running a successful business and in the past numbed himself from the stress it brought. He wanted a different path forward, one with happiness.

In one of our early sessions, I suggested Paul take a bit of time to step back and make a list of all the things he did over a couple of weeks in the business and at home. When Paul had his list, I had him step back a little further and asked if he needed to be doing all of these tasks within his business.

The answer that came to him was a game changer.

He found a lot of the items he was doing could be passed on to his employees. We came up with a plan for him to delegate these tasks. He found that not only could others do these tasks, but they were EXCITED to take them on.

Realizing that he could pass these tasks on was a lightbulb moment for Paul. Before long he was starting to find he had a bit more time. What a relief, right? You would think so but something was eating at Paul. He became uncomfortable and concerned that he might be losing control by letting go of work that he had always done. This caused him to slow down the process of allowing others to handle certain functions.

He had created some space and time for himself, but was actually starting to feel worse. We met again and Paul realized something critical: *If the business doesn't need me hands on then what will I do with my time?*

Paul realized that he did not know who he was or what he would do with himself with more time. This fear of the unknown, unless addressed would demotivate Paul from making the time he thought he wanted. Paul needed a plan for what he wanted to do with his newfound time. If he couldn't do this for himself, he would just go back to working 24/7.

The solution that we came up with together was to come up with a feasible and well-rounded plan for his life outside of work. To outline this plan, we dug deep, and I helped Paul discover, evaluate, and envision his ideal life outside of his work. We soon outlined a new plan for his ideal life and Paul put it into motion.

When Paul decided what he wanted and figured out what was holding him back, he had the opportunity to make organizational changes that could strengthen the business and create more time for him to pursue his ideal life.

By having this new plan, Paul was now able to live a more fulfilling life both inside and outside the business. In addition, his business was now more valuable and profitable as it could still successfully run with Paul being less involved, while creating more engaged employees.

Paul's story sounds straightforward, right? But it isn't and it never is. What if something else was going on?

To get where Paul is today he needed to take pause and step back and consider who he was outside the business. By doing this internal work, when the shift at work came and his time freed up, he'd be ready and excited with a plan to fill his time happily and guilt-free.

He did the work and in the process of working together, he realized it is not so much the business that needs you, it is more you need the business. He realized that his attachment to the business filled his time, gave him purpose and structure but there was more to life that he was missing out on. So taking a step back to see what else is important in life makes you more secure and allows others to help you run the business.

What would you say to me if I asked you the following questions right now?
How much do you want the business to rely on you?
What do you get out of the business needing you?
What does your responsibility in the business help you avoid?
Are there some internal shifts that may need to happen to allow the external shifts to occur?

Thinking about these questions can be both scary and intimidating.

For me, not knowing where to start kept me stuck. I kept working long hours and maintained an unhealthy lifestyle to avoid facing the hard questions instead of taking the pause, figuring out what I wanted and how to take the first steps toward achieving my ideal life.

For Paul, not having a clearly defined vision of the future held him back from fully letting others in the business help him. He still needed the business more than it needed him.

How does this all tie into creating value in the business?

What if you had to answer this question: What do you want your life to be like?

Personally, after my rock bottom moment, not all of my answers were clear. But to start, I had a strong urge to be able to actually go on vacation with my family and be there with them rather than having my head in a bottle the entire time. I imagined what this could be like, and this was enough for me to kickstart my journey.

How about you? What do you want to change in your life that would be worth making some changes in your business?

Consider:

- Is having fun with your family important to you?
- How do your social interactions feel in this ideal life?
- How do you want to feel in terms of physical fitness?
- How about your personal growth?
- How do you want to feel when you arrive home at night after a day at work?
- What might be important to you spiritually?
- What might it feel like to live exactly where you want to live?
- How do the activities and hobbies you are doing in your free time fulfill you?
- What other aspects do you want to show up in your life?

Now, imagine for a moment you answered these questions and got really clear on what you want in all the different aspects of your life. Next, visualize the power that the feeling of you living your ideal life could provide you. This is not someone else's definition of an ideal life. It's your authentic vision and your authentic power!

Now, imagine showing up at your business with this newfound sense of self. Imagine having this new energy and desire to create your life and doing the visioning work within your business that will support this.

Imagine getting things rolling and getting others involved in the process. Imagine they are now throwing ideas at you on what can be done to make things run even more smoothly. What is your business starting to feel like now? Can you get a sense of where this is all going?

This is how having the image of what you want out of life can be the ultimate value creator in your business. When you are clear on what you want, and then bring this newfound desire into the business, it is infectious. In a good way.

It has the capability to free you from the things you think only you can do and allows you the confidence and perseverance to create a company that can run without you. And a business that can run without you is one that can grow well beyond you, provide more income, as well as one that can be more easily sold or transitioned to new owners.

The work ahead will help you define success as well as help provide a framework to allow you to make it all happen.

Knowing what you want your ideal life to be like and moving toward it comes with a warning, though. Things may start going your way.

You may find yourself smiling more and appreciating the little things. You may find your business easier to run, and people within the business being more fulfilled, and taking action themselves.

If you sit back for a moment right now, in what ways can you see having a clearer vision of your ideal life impact you or your business?

• STEP BACK REFLECTION •

Looking back, can you see times in your life where you have held back from making a major change? If so what excuses have you given that helped hold you back?

_____
_____
_____
_____
_____
_____
_____
_____
_____
_____

Is there any chance the excuses you have made in the past may not be the full picture?

_____
_____
_____
_____
_____
_____
_____
_____
_____
_____

• STEP BACK REFLECTION •

If you are a business owner (or a manager of people) what may be the benefit for everyone if you were more connected to your ideal life vision? What if the people around you were more connected to their own ideal life visions?

CHAPTER 5
The Empty Teacup

It's easy to become overwhelmed by thinking about change. Regardless of what we're trying to accomplish, there are infinite ways to go about it and that can be a blessing and a curse.

As for me, one of the biggest challenges I faced was wondering, did I have it right?

After taking the step back and really doing the work on myself, I was sure that I wanted to get my MBA. When I went back to school for my MBA, I found myself reading more and more. I was a sponge.

Down this rabbit hole and then into the next, I chased new information, reading and reading and searching for new insight and answers, on the hunt for a magic bullet. I needed to find the one article (or better yet, the one sentence) that would allow everything to fall into place.

Did I just find a new rat race?

Then, my professor said something that really stuck with me.

"When you are researching information, you will come to a point of saturation when everything really just feels the same to you," he said. He went on to explain that it doesn't mean you have learned everything, but it probably means you have a solid grasp on the basic underlying principles.

I realized I had been focused on a few areas (leadership, motivation, goal setting, and organizational culture, to name a few), and I could see what he meant. I decided to take a step back and narrow my search and came to realize that I will never have all the answers. Had I waited for the perfect time, I might still be waiting. At that point, things shifted. I found a bit more peace with not having all the answers and abandoned that rat race.

Do you find yourself, from time to time, stuck in research mode?

Next, I came across the Zen concept of a beginner's mind. To be more specific, the concept encourages us to adopt a mindset where we accept that we don't have all the answers. Even now, I find myself more and more relaxing into the fact that if I adopt a beginner's mind, I don't really need to know everything. How freeing is that?

It might help to think about the teacup story:

> *Imagine for a moment you are on a search for the ultimate wisdom that has led you to a remote mountain monastery. You have been told you will meet a wise monk able to provide you great insight.*
>
> *You make the long trek to speak with the monk, and you are finally sitting across from him.*
>
> *Between the two of you is a simple table that holds two cups and a pot of tea.*
>
> *He is welcoming and asks you to introduce yourself and tell him what you seek.*
>
> *You start speaking and continue to speak and speak and speak of things you have learned, places you have been, conquests you have made. On and on, you tell him what you already know.*

> *The monk begins to pour you some tea. As he listens to you, he continues to pour the tea until the cup is overflowing.*
>
> *You stop speaking for a moment and ask him why he continues to pour the tea when your cup will clearly not hold any more.*
>
> *He stops pouring and looks you straight in the eyes and says:*
>
> *"You have come here seeking wisdom, but I am afraid it may be difficult for you to take any wisdom in. You speak and speak of all you are, all you have done, and it would appear to me that your mind is much like this teacup. Perhaps it is too full. Perhaps you may need to empty your teacup a bit so then you are able to take on more tea."*

Right about now, you are probably thinking, nice story but how does it relate to this book?

Well, sometimes we think we have all the answers and don't need any help. That's when our teacup is full.

I invite you to grab a tea, coffee, or any beverage you wish and perhaps leave a bit of room so the contents of this book may add to your cup. I invite you to enjoy the process of stepping back to get a start on the vision of your ideal self so you can go from feeling overwhelmed to feeling empowered and take the first few steps toward your ideal life.

There is no magic bullet that will make everything happen for you just by wishing and wanting it. The magic is in you, it lies in the first few small steps and your willingness to take them.

• STEP BACK REFLECTION •

What might happen if you provided more space for new learning and growth for your own journey?

Looking back, can you see times in your life where being open to new ideas has been beneficial?

CHAPTER 6

The 4 Stages of Stepping Back

Now that you understand what it means to step back and how it can help you create the life you say you want, how does it work?

What follows is an introduction to the 4-stage step back process that can be used for almost any major aspect of your life you want to improve or any change you may face.

Using the 4-stage step back process can help you:

- Find your ideal life
- Discover what those things are that make you happy
- Grow your business
- Create more time
- Reduce unhealthy stress in your life
- Expand your career
- Have a successful exit strategy

The 4-stage step back process can help you go from, "I don't know what the future holds," to a feeling of, "I know what I want the future to look and feel like, I have a plan, and I am excited to take the next step to make this a reality!"

STAGE 1: WHERE AM I RIGHT NOW? HOW ARE THINGS GOING? WHAT PROGRESS HAVE I MADE?

Do you sometimes ask yourself these questions? If so, do you find yourself feeling stuck – even paralyzed – when you think about where you are?

I sure remember how stuck I felt that morning in the detention cell. Literally and figuratively. I'd never felt so trapped.

It's not uncommon to feel stuck. The problem is if we give in to these feelings and start to become numb to the future and numb to any hope.

This is where a **growth mindset** comes in. A growth mindset is the belief that you can learn and grow, and even make mistakes, and you don't have to accept that this is all there is.

Being honest with yourself about where you are and what got you there is half the battle. Committing to the work ahead to make the change is the other half.

Once you do that, it's time to move forward.

STAGE 2: WHERE DO I WANT TO GO?

You decided it's time for a change. What is that change? This is when it's time to create a vision. In this stage, rather than limiting yourself to any overly specific outcomes, I will guide you through how creating a vision is a lot less about thinking it into reality and a lot more about tapping into what it feels like to be living a life full of meaning and purpose. A vision that fills you with a feeling of HOPE.

STAGE 3: HOW WILL I GET THERE?

Now you know where you are, and you have set a compass for where you want to go. Great. You're all set, right? Well, I would say you have some direction, but how about the road map and the gas for the car to get you there? That's what this stage is all about.

To help you on your way, you need a couple things:

Values. Your values for life allow you to better understand how you want to live every day and what is important to you in your core.

Passion. A passionate connection to your values helps you do the small things every day that will naturally allow you to create a little better version of yourself as compared to yesterday.

Purpose. It's important to uncover the different aspects of your vision and set objectives. The combination of these objectives will allow you to tap into your unique purpose.

Plan. Based on your objectives, a plan helps you tackle larger projects that will move you closer to your goals.

Perseverance. Perseverance is that feeling you get when you do something, even though it would be easier to not do it. Your passion and your purpose provide the gas for your internal engine and the plan portion gives you clarity about what to do next.

All these things come together to help you push forward!

STAGE 4: HOW DO I STAY ON TRACK?

By stage 4 in the process, you are taking action, but the journey will likely be long, filled with starts and stops, wrong turns, successes and failures. This is where patience comes in. Accept the path is going to be long, and it won't always be clear. That is key to the process.

Thinking life will instantly become what you most want is a recipe for disappointment.

Patience, on the other hand, allows us to more gracefully step into the here and now and be a bit easier on ourselves as we move forward.

Gratitude, meanwhile, allows us to appreciate the work we've done, the things we've learned, and what we already have in front of us.

Keep on track by reviewing these four stages on a regular basis. Find what works for you and understand that it really does not have to be time consuming. Aim to spend 15 minutes every week (or every couple of weeks) asking yourself where you are now, checking to ensure where you want to go is still relevant, figuring out the next steps to move forward, and thinking of ways to keep on track to create a continual improvement mindset.

I also recommend keeping a journal for your planning, reviewing and notes. It can be a great way to monitor your progress. The simple act of writing down your thoughts has wide-ranging benefits, from decluttering your thoughts to allowing you to set your targets for the day to move toward your ideal life.

• STEP BACK REFLECTION •

Take a moment here to press pause and jot down some brief initial thoughts to the questions below regarding either your life, your business or career

Where are you now?

_____
_____
_____
_____
_____
_____
_____
_____
_____
_____

Where do you want to go?

_____
_____
_____
_____
_____
_____
_____
_____
_____
_____

• STEP BACK REFLECTION •

How will you get there?

_____
_____
_____
_____
_____
_____
_____
_____

How will you keep on track?

_____
_____
_____
_____
_____
_____
_____
_____
_____
_____
_____

CHAPTER 7
Stage One – Calling Out Change

Where are you now?

Did something lead you to pick up this book? Are you on the brink of change? Or do you want to create that change?

To create change we need to ask ourselves: *'What is going on in my life or my business that I want to be different?'*

When we think about change it doesn't have to be negative. Creating change is hard, but it doesn't always have a negative impact on our lives. Instead growth, happiness, success and more can be the result of change.

Change is difficult because we have been the way we currently are for a long time and our habits are deeply ingrained. Our ability to find and maintain motivation and a positive mindset for meaningful and long-lasting change will ultimately determine whether we are able to break long-standing habits and patterns.

But, adopting a **POSITIVE GROWTH MINDSET,** will help you generate a positive outcome out of change. It will even make the whole process of change easier on you. Why fight it with negativity?

Stage 1 is about calling out what it is that you want to change, then taking time to prepare for the work ahead.

A few questions can be used for any major change to help you set yourself up for more success. Let's use the earlier coaching conversation from chapter two as an example.

Question 1: Can you describe, as objectively as possible, the situation you find yourself in that you want to change? What are the facts a reporter or journalist would observe?

The point of this question is to uncover the real facts of your situation, versus what you may be feeling or telling yourself about them.

Here's an example:

> *Business owner reports he would like to spend more time with the family. He owns a business that is making a profit of $300,000 per year after paying himself $150,000 per year. He spends 10-12 hours at work each workday, and 4 hours working on Saturday. At home, he's tired and prefers to sit alone watching TV. His family appears to largely live their own lives and interaction between family members is limited.*

As you can see here, we're not reading into the situation, we're just reciting the facts. This forces you to remove yourself from the situation and observe it as if you had no emotional connection. This allows you to better see the situation from a different perspective.

Question 2: What do you tell yourself about this situation?

Now that you have the facts, it's time to dig deeper. What is the story that you tell yourself about the situation and the possible change you want to make?

Here's another example:

> *How do I even start to make this change? It feels overwhelming! I have to work all these hours because I am the only one capable of doing this work! When I look even further into the future, what is the point? My family doesn't want me around anyway. How could I have let this happen to me? It's hopeless. I am such a loser.*

Does any of this sound familiar to stories you tell yourself? If so, don't fear. You are not alone. Many people follow a path of negative self-talk. Before long, we can fall into self-loathing and pity, finding ourselves feeling even more stuck. Becoming aware that we do this and noticing when it comes up in our minds are huge steps forward.

Take the time to step back and ask yourself, what is the story I am telling myself about this situation? Then look at the actual situation.

Question 3: Do you really believe these stories you are telling yourself? Do the facts of the story match what you're saying? If you were talking to someone else in the same situation, what would you say to them? What story would you rather be telling yourself?

Imagine you're coaching someone else, a person you love. You don't have to sugar coat it and not everyone has to get a trophy. But how would you speak to them about what is going on? Try to use that voice for yourself and come up with a more objective statement regarding the situation and what you can do about it.

For instance:

> *I want to spend more time with my family, and it's true I feel a*

> *distance between us. But I can have a conversation with them. I have that capability, and things are not so far gone that they left. I can make things right. I can also start looking at what it is in the business I think only I can do and see if this is true. I'm a good person who has created a very successful company, and I am sure if I put the same effort into this situation, I can make positive changes here as well.*

As you can see in this example, taking a step back and comparing the facts to the stories you tell yourself and applying some compassion helps you change the story in your mind. It may seem too easy, but I encourage you to try this technique a few times and see what it does for you.

Once you have a better idea of what the actual situation is and have a more empowering internal story behind it, it's time to look a little more at the situation to see what internal shifts may be ahead for you.

Question 4: What is it you want to change internally, embrace, or let go of so you can take the next steps in creating your ideal life, business or whatever else you want to change?

We can all learn and grow and often that process confronts us with uncomfortable thoughts or emotions inside of us.

Consider this example:

> *As the business owner looked deeper into the fear of his family not wanting him around, he realized that he needed to have a conversation with them. Looking deeper, he found he was resisting this conversation. He had been brought up with the idea that men do not talk about their feelings and they just*

"had all the answers." This was modeled to him by his father and other male role models in his life, and over time, he had adopted this as his working model of the world. Through some work with his coach, he was able to embrace a new belief that it's OK to not have all the answers. This allowed him a lot of freedom in his life. He was able to start the conversation with his wife about what it would be like if he was to spend more time with the family. He was also able to start looking for people who, like him, would not have all the answers but could help him out more at the business.

As you can see, there can often be both external and internal shifts that surface as you dive deeper into the change process.

If right about now you feel a bit overwhelmed, I invite you to simply exhale and then take a few long slow deep breaths.

Change can be a challenging process. At the same time, it can also be exciting and fulfilling. A key thing to embrace is that small steps, consistently taken, eventually get you to your destination.

The more you can adopt a POSITIVE GROWTH MINDSET, the more likely you will be to transform your life, business, or any other challenge.

Remind yourself daily that a positive growth mindset allows you to be the person who can make the changes you want to make, keep learning, grow beyond where you are, and achieve your dreams.

"In a growth mindset, people believe that their most basic abilities can be developed through dedication and hard work—brains and talent are just the starting point," writes Carol Dweck, a psychologist and author of *Mindset: The New Psychology of Success*. "This view creates a love of learning and a resilience that is essential for great accomplishment."* Dweck explains how people can either adopt a growth mindset (growth intelligence mindset) or a fixed mindset (fixed intelligence mindset).

A fixed mindset is where you may think that you are who you are at birth and there is nothing you can do to change the cards you have been dealt. In this mindset you would have a belief that your intelligence, and underlying capabilities are the limits of your growth.

On the other hand, if you have a belief of a growth mindset you will think that you can increase your intelligence with effort, and that over time you can develop and stretch your capabilities.** In short, a growth mindset means you can grow beyond what nature has provided you with effort and deliberate practice.

In her two decades of research, Dweck discovered that the view you choose to embrace for yourself deeply affects how you live your life, determining whether you become who you want to be and whether you achieve what you value.

The image on the next page is a great way to work through what adopting a growth mindset means as opposed to settling for a fixed mindset.***

---

* Juma, Norbert, "40 Carol Dweck Quotes About A Growth Mindset," Everyday Power, April 8, 2020. https://everydaypower.com/carol-dweck-quotes/

** "Carol Dweck on Fixed Mindset vs. Growth Mindset." Examined Existence. Accessed September 22, 2020. https://examinedexistence.com/carol-dweck-on-fixed-mindset-vs-growth-mindset/.

***"The Impact of a Growth Mindset," Science Impact. Accessed September 18, 2020. https://www.mindsetworks.com/science/Impact.

As for me, my first step was to convince myself that I really could make changes in my life. This mindset helped me see that I could take control and move forward.

I could have chosen to stay with the business I was already in. That life offered the comfort of the money. But, if I stayed I would have had to pretend that the numbing effect of the booze was enough to get me through the stress and the longing for something more. Instead, I left that life and chose to grow. The sense that there was something more was too powerful to ignore, and I embraced a growth mindset that allowed me to step into the unknown!

When I decided to go back to school in 2012, the prerequisite for most MBA programs was an undergrad degree. That was a problem. I didn't have one, but I decided it wouldn't stop me. I wanted to go back to school, and in fact, I felt I needed to go back. I needed to grow and my passion to move forward pushed me through. I found a couple of programs that would accept high scores on a qualifying exam (GMAT) with prior business experience.

Studying for the GMAT was brutal. I had been out of school for 20+ years. I had to relearn tons of topics from basic grammar to statistics, all of which somehow had snuck out of my head since I studied them before. There were many times when I didn't understand the information and at many points I could have easily thrown in the towel.

I kept going forward, though. It took effort and dedication, and, in the end, I studied hard, achieved the mark I needed for the GMAT, had the entrance interview, and was accepted!

What was the key that fueled my progress through this experience? You guessed it. Mindset! I believed I could learn and grow. I am pretty sure it was the pride when I finally learned a subject, and it clicked, that really pushed me to learn the next subject.

To reinforce the power of adopting a growth mindset, I would like to introduce another concept.

Remember me sitting at my desk having a drink? I thought there was no one out there who could help me run the business. I thought I had to do it all myself. I pointed my finger at where the business was located, blaming my problems on people within the company not wanting to take on more responsibility, and even blaming society for not helping create the exact right person to help me out! I blamed the situation on everything but me. I was not willing to look deeper into myself at this point of my life.

Then I read a book recommended by one of my coach friends, Dan Ohler: *The Power of TED (The Empowerment Dynamic)* by David Emerald.

Emerald describes how we have the choice between two ways of being in this world. The first is to choose to be a **victim**, one I was making so well. In short, a victim feels someone or something is persecuting them, and they need someone or something to rescue them from it. Nothing is their fault, and nothing is really in their control.

The book goes on to describe, and some would say prescribe, the antidote, which is to choose the mindset of the **creator**. From here, we can see that it is up to us to respond to situations with an open and solutions-focused mindset. The creator empowers him/herself with possibilities and then accepts help from others. Whether it is them being open to feedback or asking people for help or even reading books, the creator feels empowered to move forward.

You can see how the positive growth mindset and creator mindset are closely linked. Ultimately, by adopting these mindsets, you will believe you can grow and learn and that you are the one in the driver's seat to make it happen.

CASE STUDY | MEET STAN

As the owner of a thriving industrial business, Stan was stressed out, sleepwalking through his life, addicted to drugs, distant, unable to ask for help, and disconnected from any kind of power larger than himself.

After watching his dad's repeated bouts with cancer, Stan realized that he himself was living in unhealthy ways.

I met Stan shortly after he said yes to treatment for alcohol and drug addiction in 2015. Two essential questions became his guide for moving forward:

Who am I and how do I fit into this world?

He was ready to make changes in his life that would create a new legacy for himself and his own family, but he didn't know how to do it. That is where I stepped in.

We had a lot in common. I was able to be a role model for him while coaching him one-on-one for several months.

During our sessions, we addressed Stan's fears about the future and his limiting beliefs. Next, I helped Stan come up with a practical game plan to make this happen.

The biggest thing I helped Stan with was listening and asking powerful questions that really allowed him to do the hard work of evaluating his future options. My questions helped Stan develop a growth mindset.

Stan made a decision to change his life. Looking back, he saw that if he didn't have my support as a coach, he might have gone back to his old work, and maybe even to drinking or using drugs again.

Finding his business vision

One of the critical aspects that we looked at was Stan's business. He wondered if engineering was still what he wanted to do. I helped him explore other options and what it was that was leading him to question his current career path.

By working with me, Stan was able to look at the entire system of his life. This led him to begin tapping into what he wanted in aspects such as family, friends, physical health, and spirituality. He soon was able to see that his current business was conflicting with these other aspects.

During one of our last sessions together, he told me that I was a constant beacon and source of support. It was through our coaching and sessions that he was able to commit to doing something new, going back to school, and leaving behind a business that was no longer serving his passion and purpose in life. Now Stan is a certified Health & Lifestyle Coach with a thriving practice driven by his passion for changing the health and consciousness of the planet through changing habits.

What is your attitude toward change right now? How are you feeling about your mindset at this point? Do you feel you have a growth and a creator's mindset? Would you like to adopt more of a growth mindset or a creator's mindset into your life? Are you wondering just how you can do this? Let me help.

Becoming aware of what you are thinking during challenging situations is a way of tapping into your growth mindset. The next time you find yourself facing a challenge or are frustrated with yourself, take a few moments to breathe. Let whatever emotions come up to just be present for a minute or so. Just sit with whatever you are feeling and simply breathe in and out through your nose. You should feel calmer and more open after a few rounds of breathing. This will allow you to now face challenges rather than to avoid them because of potential difficult emotions. Using this small growth mindset technique will allow you to take a step back, gain calmness, and be able to approach any situation with a sense of clarity, openness, and excitement.

For me, taking a step back and breathing and allowing myself to feel what is going on has been a game-changer. It has allowed me to live a life of responding rather than reacting in difficult situations. I have been doing this growth mindset breathing technique for years and it was a cool experience to see a similar technique discussed and explained in Dr. Joan Rosenberg's book, *90 Seconds To A Life You Love*.

Dr. Joan Rosenberg, creator of the Rosenberg reset reinforced the power of how sitting with difficult emotions for 90 seconds on an ongoing basis can help us build confidence, reduce anxiety, and help us move toward a life we love.

Once you are a bit calmer, work through the questions below:

- Can you describe, as objectively as possible, the situation you want to change?
- What is it that you might be telling yourself about this situation?
- Do you fully believe that what you are telling yourself is based on facts?

- Do the facts of the story match your inner dialogue?
- If you were talking to a real friend in the same situation, how would you speak to them?
- What would be more beneficial to tell yourself?
- What is it you may want to change internally, embrace, or let go of so you can take the next steps in creating your ideal life, business or whatever else you want to change?

When you notice your thoughts and reflect on them, you can transform the story. You are using practical mindfulness instead of allowing negative thoughts to hijack your emotions.

Essentially, when you step away and take pause you are removing yourself from what *is*. You are giving yourself the space to consciously be alone with your thoughts to reflect. Asking yourself the deeper questions. This is intentional and very powerful – because it is in this space of practicing mindfulness that you can further develop a growth- and creator-focused mindset. As you practice mindfulness activities, many of which I offer here, you will deepen your growth- and creator-focused mindset. This will help you notice the small situations as they come up through the day until practice makes it a habit! You can ask yourself, "What would I do with this from a growth or creator's mindset?" Life happens fast but if we can just step back for a few seconds we have the ability to create our own future.

Consider these two similar scenarios:

> *You're driving in your car. Someone roars up behind you and is right on your tail. They are honking. You react. Instantly you are mad, and everything is on this driver. You start yelling, and as he tries to pass, you swerve to block him. He finally gets past as you flip him off. All throughout the day, you relive this moment telling others about it and how it is this driver's fault that you are angry and frustrated. You eventually go home, kick the cat, and get into a fight with your better half...*
>
> *You are driving in your car. Someone roars up behind you and is right on your tail. They are honking. You feel yourself getting frustrated, but instead of reacting you pause just for a second. You look at your speedometer and notice you are just under the speed limit. You think they must be in a hurry, so you pull over to let them pass. Perhaps they were on the way to a hospital. You let the situation go and carry on having a great day. At the end of the day you go home, you pet the cat, and have a lovely evening with your better half.*

I hope you can see from this simple example how pausing can make a huge impact on your day. So, how might this apply to your life, your business or your business transition? How can stepping back and spending time in mindful reflection impact you and the creation of your future?

It helps to keep a log of your habits and actions when you go through a change. I use this technique when I am facing a large change, as well as reflecting on how I've reacted (sometimes poorly) to certain situations. I also use it when I find myself a little low and realize I'm telling myself a negative story.

This simple technique of keeping a log of your habits and actions is also beneficial when you find yourself upset or triggered by something. When you find yourself judging another person or situation harshly. It's often at these times that we need to look at what is really going on. Most of the time it's more about you than them.

Are you feeling more inspired? Do you have the feeling you can move forward in this process and that you can learn, grow, and create your ideal situation? I hope so because you can! There is so much potential for growth and creation right there inside of you, inside of us all.

• BONUS: INNER VOICE WORKSHEET •

Please visit
www.daveinclair.ca/numbbustingresources
to download a worksheet you can use to go through the process to help you become aware of your inner voice and start taking steps to have it working for you!

• STEP BACK REFLECTION •

In the last couple of weeks can you see a situation where adopting a growth, or creator's mindset may have been to your benefit?

_____
_____
_____
_____
_____
_____
_____
_____

Can you think of a time in the last couple of weeks, where being more aware of your thoughts and responding rather than reacting, may have helped you or others around you?

_____
_____
_____
_____
_____
_____
_____
_____
_____
_____

CHAPTER 8

Stage Two – Visualizing an Oasis in the Desert

Where do you want to go?

You have taken a step back and looked at where you are, and have explored your current mindset. Now it is time to decide where you want to go.

One of the first steps of any journey is deciding on your destination. In this case, it means asking yourself: Where do I want to go?

Step away from everything for a few moments, close your eyes and tap into what matters to you most. What do you miss that you wish you could attract back into your life? What is calling you? How do you want your life to look two years from now, five years from now and in 10 years? Now, do you remember what we talked about in the last chapter? About growth and creator mindsets? Having the life you want is within your control.

When I did this work, I knew I wanted to create a life where I would feel good about how I was living and where I was headed. By no means did I have it all figured out, but envisioning my new ideal self through the power of belief, growth and creation empowered me to start toward this future. The step back process was how I became aware of, and started believing in my abilities, and acted upon my vision for my future. It was and still is, my empowered journey.

The rest of the details would develop over time, and to be honest, they continue to develop to this day. That is the beauty of the step back process. It can keep serving you as you learn more about what is important to you.

So why do it? Why create a vision?

Think about these two, very different scenarios:

> *You are leaving for an unknown destination sometime in the next three weeks. You might be gone for as little as two days or up to three months. You haven't arranged accommodations. What do you notice going on in your stomach? Are you starting to get a bit anxious? (I know I would be.)*
>
> *Now, you are going to go on a vacation to Venice in six months for three weeks. You've booked your tickets and accommodation near your favorite bistro overlooking the water. You've also planned a few activities to do when you are there. What does this feel like?*

How does having a vision of your trip affect your overall confidence? Does it help you create a plan? Does it help you take steps to get there? Does it change how you might respond to someone asking about your upcoming trip?

Going through the process of envisioning a well-rounded future allows you to tap into what is important to you and what really matters in your life, your business or the transition.

STAGE TWO – VISUALIZING AN OASIS IN THE DESERT

CASE STUDY | MEET CHARLIE

I met Charlie as he was trying to start up his business.

Born in Africa, Charlie was abandoned as a child and was a war survivor. This early life brought him into an early adulthood filled with scars and a sense of hopelessness.

Charlie heard my lecture at a local college. He had been searching for a way to heal his heart and to help the people in his home country. He just didn't know where to go. My message resonated with him, and soon after, we began to work together.

During our coaching sessions, Charlie discovered he could change the old, negative beliefs in his head by listening to himself and by creating a new mindset. I helped him discover how to ask himself questions around what he ideally wanted in life and how to find the answers for himself.

Because Charlie's past experiences had been so negative, we worked to change the negative thought patterns that came from them. He felt like he'd started a fresh page in his life.

Charlie also took the time in our sessions, and between them to create a well-rounded vision for his future. I guided in helping him find within himself what he wanted and why he wanted it. This was a turning point for him. One that allowed Charlie to tap into his own unique sense of purpose for his life and to set out for this ultimate destination. He soon learned that he could impact others in a positive way, as much as himself, and gained a new sense of balance.

It wasn't long until Charlie became a social entrepreneur. He started a company that sources markets for goods that are made in his home country. He set up the company with the purpose of supporting people from his home country by importing products that he believes in, and this brings him great satisfaction.

I've found what matters to most of my clients (and me, too) are the things that fill us up from the inside rather than from the outside. For Charlie that was helping his home country while still becoming an entrepreneur.

Why is it important to focus on what fills us up on the inside? Because once you focus on your inner self, the rest of your life starts to make more sense.

Taking the time to step back and figure out what is important to you can have some pretty remarkable results.

We often think we want too much. *It can make us feel guilty. This is not always the challenge. Why shouldn't we have all that our hearts desire?* ***The real question is what is YOUR all? YOUR all that will lead you to an inner state of fulfillment, purpose and meaning.***

I invite you to pause for a moment here. What is your all? If you could open the book of your life right now to the page that said "My all" what are the words or phrases that would be written on there?

For me these words would be: fulfillment, connection, contribution, happiness and peace.

Once I realized I needed to focus on these internal states of being rather than the things that make me temporarily happy, things started to make more sense.

Don't just take my word for it, though.

In a 1996 study, Tim Kasser and Richard M. Ryan found that people who focus on intrinsic goals (affiliation, community feeling, physical fitness, and self-acceptance) that satisfy basic human and psychological needs are healthier and experience overall higher levels of well-being and less distress compared to people who have goals that are primarily extrinsic (financial success, social recognition, and physical appearance).[*]

	INCREASES	DECREASES
Higher focus on intrinsic aspirations	Self-actualization and vitality	Depression
Higher focus on extrinsic aspirations	Negative Physical symptoms	Self-actualization and vitality
Belief your intrinsic goals are possible	Self-actualization and vitality	Depression
Belief in your extrinsic goals are possible	Depression	Self-actualization and vitality
Adopting Intrinsic guiding principles	Self-actualization	Negative Physical symptoms
Adopting Extrinsic guiding principles	Negative Physical symptoms	Self-actualization

---

[*] Kasser, Tim, and Ryan, Richard M., "Further Examining the American Dream: Differential Correlates of Intrinsic and Extrinsic Goals," *Personality and Social Psychology Bulletin*, 22:3 (March 1996): 280-287

What does this mean? It means that focusing on what is meaningful to you is important. Focusing on intrinsic goals can also increase your overall well-being and satisfaction in life, according to the study.

In practical terms, it is important not to just think of money as the main object when you are setting goals of any kind. Money and work are important aspects of our life. However, if you want to live a happier and more fulfilling life, you will need to figure out other meaningful goals that allow you to create a well-rounded vision of success.

CASE STUDY | MEET MIKE

I coached a business owner named Mike who wanted to find a new owner for his business. We met a few times, and he wanted to jump right into the nuts and bolts of finding this new owner so he could be financially able to "live his life."

In one of our earlier meetings, I asked Mike what he imagined his new life would look like after selling the business to which he responded, "well, I can see myself relaxing in a chair."

I asked him what it was like to be there, and why this was important to him. This question caused him to sink into the feeling more and more. Then we started to explore what it was that was allowing him to sit so comfortably in that chair.

Mike explained that to maintain family harmony throughout the transition would allow him to rest comfortably and feel secure that his family would be a big part of his life. That intrinsic goal allowed him to gain overall life satisfaction.

Here are some comparable goals to consider as you envision your own future:

> **YOUR PERSONAL LIFE**
> - Increase the quality time spent with friends and family
> - Work toward completing a marathon
> - Improve communication with my spouse
> - Meditate on a daily basis
>
> **YOUR BUSINESS**
> - Create a culture where everyone feels they are contributing
> - Ensure customers see value beyond the price they pay for products
> - Support a charity that is meaningful to the company
> - Operate at a profit and take care of stakeholders
>
> **YOUR BUSINESS TRANSITION**
> - Ensure the transition allows you to fully step into your life outside the business
> - Set up the transition to ensure the business survives beyond the sale
> - Ensure a transition affects employees in a positive way

This is about you finding your own answers. To help you see what you will create for yourself throughout the second part of this book please refer to my sample ideal life vision wheel on the next page.

As you look at the diagram, you may have a few questions. I'm often asked if it's important for everyone to include all of these categories. The simple answer is, no, it's your vision. All that matters is that the aspects you select are right for you.

You may look at this and think "What if I cannot get clear on all the different aspects of my life all at once?". That is OK. In fact it is quite normal. I tell people, as I also view my life vision this way, that it is always a work in progress. Start now and keep coming back to fill in the blanks or modify it.

MY DEFINITION OF SUCCESS

- **Where we live-** We are living in a nice house with a built in greenhouse. We overlook a wonderful spot in nature, and are able to exercise outside all year, We are close to town, yet have the privacy we need to connect with nature.

- **My work-** My mission is to help individuals and organizations first define what success is to them and to empower them to create their own road map to achieve this. This work feeds my soul, provides abundant security, while I work 16-24 hours per week

- **Giving Back-** I continue to mentor, guide, and coach people meeting them where they are. I facilitate a men's group to aid those faced with varying forms of addiction.

- **Financial Security-** I can look at our investments, savings, and bank account and know our financial future is well taken care of

- **Gaylene-** Love. Harmony. Teamwork. Passion. My soulmate. Our own lives as individuals together. We are bulletproof

- **Recreation-** We are taking a few of trips per year and have fulfilling hobbies

- **Growth-** I am taking in the small moments allowing them to further develop my positive mental foundation. I read, learn, and share topics that are of interest to me and that can further support mankind.

- **Family and Friends-** I am connecting and spending time with people I love, and they love me. This provides a deep feeling of human connection.

- **Spirituality-** I am continually awakening to the future that I am a part of. I do this through the small wonders in the world that I can learn from. Patience is my guide, fulfilled balance is my goal, and mindfulness is my path.

- **Health-** I am happy, healthy and having fun. I am around 200#s and able to run a half marathon whenever I want to, I am an inspiration to others.

You may also get the impression that you need to have your life perfectly divided among these different areas. That's not the case. Instead, the vision and the goals you have in each segment are here to help ground you in what you would like to work toward in your life. It can help you tap into a well-rounded sense of purpose.

My goal is that you have a tangible takeaway—a vision that is custom-suited to you and your objectives—that you can then refer back to regularly as you move forward.

• STEP BACK REFLECTION •

Looking ahead, how might having a well-rounded vision of your life, and how you would like to show up in the different aspects of your life, assist you?

CHAPTER 9

Stage Three – One Bite at a Time

Now that you have your vision, you might want to tackle every area right away. How does that feel? If you're anything like me, it may feel almost impossible! Where the hell do you start?

Often this is where things may start to fall apart. The to-do list seems just too huge, like an elephant. And how do you eat an elephant? Most people will tell you to do it one bite at a time. And they're not wrong, but that's still a lot of bites.

I say you need to build up an appetite first. This is where passion and purpose come in.

Passion, as defined by Merriam-Webster is the "continued effort to do or achieve something despite difficulties, failure, or opposition." It is the feel-good feeling that you get when you put your mind to something important to you, and this increases your excitement to get to it!

Purpose, as defined by Merriam-Webster is "the feeling of being determined to do or achieve something." Purpose provides the long-term appetite that will get you to where you want to go.

Still a little muddy? Let's go a little deeper.

To me, passion is the feeling I get from knowing I am living truer to my authentic self and what I deem important in my life. From enjoying the views and the crisp air on my morning run, to planning a trip to Sedona with my wife. It's the feeling I get when I sit down with a good book or take the time to make a healthy and delicious meal. Passion is being in the here and now with all the things that fuel my soul, and that I know are good for me, allowing me to better enjoy the journey to wherever it is I am headed.

When we tap into what is truly important, it clears the picture of what we value. Our values drive our passion. In your personal life, your business or even your business transition, tapping into what you value is key to ensuring you can do what you are doing with passion.

Purpose is the underlying push that feeds you and helps you master your long-term goals. It is the feeling that you get that what you are doing matters.

So, what if you can't come up with a single purpose or mission statement? Not to worry, in fact I find this is quite common. There is a lot we learn in school but we were never expected to create a purpose or mission statement for our life. This is where the step back process helps. By defining what we want for the different areas of our lives, as well as how we want to feel in these areas we create an overall well-rounded sense of purpose in our life.

Consider the vision wheel from the previous chapter. I took time to write objectives and descriptions for each segment. These act like mini purpose statements that, when combined, give my entire life an overall sense of purpose.

This process will allow you to create a sense of passion and purpose that is custom-tailored to your own definition of success!

This is an exciting step in the journey, because so many of us have walked around our entire lives without asking of ourselves what really matters to us. No wonder we're unfulfilled and overworked!

Finding your purpose feeds the soul and makes you want to commit to the actions you'll take to make this life you dream of happen.

Finding your passion allows you to better connect with what's important to you on a daily basis as you drive toward mastering your goals. This allows you to enjoy the journey as well as the destination.

Now that you have your appetite, we still need a plan on how to eat that elephant!

WHY YOU NEED A PLAN

If you really want to turn your life into the stuff of your dreams, incorporating these steps is a proven way to get there:

1. Fully think through your goals
2. Write down your goals
3. Create action steps to make the goals happen
4. Share these goals and action steps with someone who will support you along the way
5. Create accountability by reporting back to them on a regular basis

---

Gail Matthews, a Professor of Psychology at Dominican University of California conducted a study on the way these five support mechanisms increase people's ability to achieve their goals. She found that people who followed just the first step (thinking through their goal) achieved their goal 42% of the time. Using all five steps nearly doubled the likelihood of completing the goal—to 76%.

Let's imagine, for example, that you have a goal to build a company that will be valued at and eventually sold for $5,000,000 and that this goal is a key long-range plan for your business to build your retirement fund. Can you afford to and are you willing to leave this plan to chance?

When you back up what you want and what you are willing and able to do with passion and purpose, these elements enhance the nature of the process. If personal development and growth could increase your odds of reaching any goal you set from 42% to 76%, would you invest in that?

When a person develops their passion and purpose behind their "why" the process of working toward a goal takes on the added dimension of ease and excitement. Purpose, passion and perseverance make the goal feasible and sustains the vision for the goal-setter; in this case – the plan to grow a company to $5,000,000 and then sell as a retirement fund.

Perseverance is defined by Merriam-Webster as the "continued effort to do or achieve something despite difficulties, failure, or opposition."

I would say that perseverance is the magic that happens when you have a growth mindset, vision of the future, passion, purpose, and a plan combined. It allows you to carry on beyond the failures and the hard times. Perseverance is that feeling you get that tells you to get your butt out of bed and do the things you need to do. To do the best you can in the moment and to battle past the voices in your head saying it is too hard.

Angela Duckworth, author the instant New York Times bestseller *Grit: The Power of Passion and Perseverance* studied these in depth. Her findings show that a combination of passion and perseverance for an important goal – she calls it grit – is the hallmark of high achievers. Grit, it turns out, is the key determinant of whether high achievers reach their goal.

I facilitate a men's group for addiction recovery, and it's amazing to walk alongside these fantastic men as they share their ups and downs. One thing consistently shows up, though; the men who do best are the ones who exhibit perseverance. The perseverant men continuously show up and talk about the plan they are working to stay with their program. These are the men who talk with passion and purpose and how they are connected to what they value. These are the men who become the role models for others in the group. It is these men who have learned that the only way forward is to persevere.

Allow me to introduce just one more concept in this chapter that is a game changing one. Do you remember when I asked: 'how do you eat an elephant?' One bite at a time?

As you begin to build your plan, you might find that you easily get lost in many different projects, trying to bite off more than you can chew. The key game-changing decision that you can make is to start by selecting the one thing, that one bite, that will make the biggest difference.

In their book *The One Thing: The Surprisingly Simple Truth behind Extraordinary Results*, authors Gary Keller and Jay Papasan describe the "one thing" as the project, action step, or clarification that when you have completed it will make everything else easier or not even required. This means stepping back to determine the most critical thing to do right now, so that by doing it, it will have the biggest impact overall.

That one thing is both a compass and a roadmap, according to Keller and Papasan. The compass functions as your overall vision, your passion and your purpose. It's the 20,000-foot overhead view of what you want to accomplish, how you will do it, and why it is really important to you.

The roadmap is for you to start making it all happen. Where will you start? And what will be the next waypoint?

I have worked with people who started with creating a list of core objectives for their business transition and others who created a business plan that empowers them to start a business. I've helped clients create a business strategy to transition them out of roles, as well as helped people put self-care plans in place. I have even helped people form business plans that ended up showing them that they didn't want to start the business after all.

The choices are endless, and at the end of the day, the step back process will help you create your compass, roadmap, and will help you zero in on the one thing you need to start with so you can move forward.

CASE STUDY | MEET CHELSEY

Chelsey moved to Canada from Germany, where she had spent her career in the hospitality business. Her work involved lots of world travel and interactions with other people.

After relocating to Canada for her husband's new job, Chelsey went to work for a nonprofit that helps immigrant populations adapt and grow in their new country. The work fit her so well that she eventually became a certified parent coach, guiding families around how to live more successful lives.

Chelsey decided that coaching would help her refine her vision and grow beyond the fears she still had about branching out on her own. She started working with me to help her find a solution.

Through coaching, Chelsey learned how to be more curious about herself by asking questions. I began helping her understand why she wants to do the things she dreams of and how she can find more courage to move forward with the steps it will take to get there. During our one-on-one sessions, she came to realize her insecurities could become opportunities.

She said she credits me with this insight as it is now a driving motivation for her coaching business. In her mind, everyone has strengths, and she wants to inspire people to see that in themselves.

Chelsey has moved forward in many ways to build her new career. Her biggest dream is to open a space where she can meet her clients. She sees it as having a very European feel, with a focus on quality and details that incorporate everything that has made her life so rich.

• STEP BACK REFLECTION •

Can you recall times in your life when passion, purpose and perseverance were more alive in you? What lesson is there for you right now in how you can bring more of this back into your present life?

_____
_____
_____
_____
_____
_____
_____
_____
_____

Off the top of your head, what is one thing that would make the biggest difference in your life, career, or business?

_____
_____
_____
_____
_____
_____
_____
_____
_____
_____

• STEP BACK REFLECTION •

How might passion, purpose, and planning help you with one change you have wanted to make in your life, your career, or your business?

CHAPTER 10
Stage Four – Prepare to Enjoy the Marathon

You know where you are and where you want to go. You've adopted a growth mindset and have the passion, purpose, plan and perseverance to get there. All done, right?

Close. But there's one more lesson, and this lesson is integral to learning how to stay on course.

Anything worth doing often takes time. Remember there are no magic bullets, and it is more like a marathon than a sprint. This is where patience and gratitude fit in.

For instance, I think of the first marathon I ran. I trained for it, worked hard at it, and completed it. It was tough, and I felt like giving up many times during the race as well as the training leading up to it.

Why do I bring this up? I bring it up because of what kept me going: **Gratitude and patience.**

Gratitude opens space for us to step back and appreciate what is here now. It is gratitude for my body that allows me to run, gratitude for the miles I have put in during training, and for what I have learned that allows me to smile as I am taking the steps. Shifting my thoughts from, "Oh crap, this run is sucking right now," to "I am grateful to be able to move my body," helps me persevere in the times I need a little extra encouragement.

Patience is what allows us to be a bit gentler and kinder to ourselves as we progress on our journey.

The need for patience became very clear to me during my marathon run. When the run started, I was excited. I trained for a long time leading up to it and I had a goal in mind. I figured I could finish in 3 hours 45 minutes, and my target was 4 hours. Not super-fast but respectable.

I found a pack of people whose pace felt right for my timing, and off I went. I felt good. I felt REALLY good. You could even say I was fast. Then things started to unravel.

At the 10 kilometer mark, I looked at my stopwatch and saw I was at 50 minutes, way ahead of my target pace. Although you may think that was great, I realized things were amiss. I checked in on my breathing and my body and saw I was not where I needed to be. I was already feeling my legs tire and my breath was labored. I was trying way too hard.

I slowed things down a bit, but was still laboring by the mid-way mark in the race. I could have easily pulled out at that point and quit, but I carried on. I had to slow down a lot and started having some pretty bad stomach cramps. I had taken some extra electrolytes, which I had never taken before, to help give me a boost. Only there's no such thing as a magic bullet, right?

I remember at one point passing someone on the side who was receiving serious medical attention. This really struck me, and I remember thinking, "Dave it's not worth it. Finish, but don't kill yourself." I refocused, felt grateful to be where I was, and finished the last 15 kilometers running and walking. It was all I could do, but I did it, and I didn't die. I crossed the line just under 4 hours 30 minutes, well over my goal time but I still felt accomplished. I knew what it took for me to get there and it was still amazing.

This is when I understood and gained an appreciation for patience. Yes, it's good to have a goal, Yes, it's great to move toward it, but it might not go 100% to plan and we have to learn to be patient and forgiving with ourselves and our goals. Maybe today's marathon wasn't it for me and I can wait for the next one, I can try again to meet that goal. Learn, and grow.

Other lessons from the marathon? Stick with your plan and run your race. Do what you can to get to the end, but don't sacrifice everything else to get there. Have goals but also hold onto them a little more lightly. Adopting this mindset allows you to flex and shift as you move forward, learn and grow.

Take your time.

Once we become impassioned by our own vision of how things can be, it's natural to want it to happen now. But life is not a sprint. It's a marathon. So take a moment to catch your breath and settle in for a nice slow, steady run. Be patient and enjoy it.

If you can cultivate patience, flexibility, trust in the process and enjoy the steps you take, you will also cultivate the ability to get out of your own way.

In the step back process, if a new idea or a new way, comes to you, trust it. Even if the steps take you in the wrong direction, trust that what you will learn will help you with the next step. Remember, you can always go back to where you were, adjust, and now move forward with your new insights

As you complete the steps, test to see if you feel you are on track, adjust as needed, and take some more. This is key. The step back process is not meant to be done just once; it's a way to live by moving forward.

One of the easiest ways to maintain a positive mindset, enjoy the journey, and keep on track is to express gratitude for the progress you have made, and what you have in your life. From the smell of your morning coffee and positive interactions with people in your business to sitting back and smiling when you complete the first step in a project, gratitude changes you.

• BONUS •

For a free exercise on how to further practice gratitude visit
www.davesinclair.ca/numbbustingresources now!

• STEP BACK REFLECTION •

What are three things you are grateful for in your life?

_____
_____
_____
_____
_____
_____
_____
_____
_____
_____
_____

In what ways can bringing more patience into your life benefit you, and those around you?

_____
_____
_____
_____
_____
_____
_____
_____
_____
_____
_____

CHAPTER 11

Step Back in Your Daily Life... Let It Sink In

The process ahead is not just for the big projects in your life, but can also be practiced with the small everyday things in your life! In chapter 11 we will talk about a few of the ways you can take pause and step back in your day to day life.

As for me, taking stock of where I am right now has allowed me to check in on my progress and learn from my actions and the information it provides. By checking in, I can ensure that I am living true to myself and work on continuing to take those steps toward where I want to go.

I also often find myself stepping back and checking in when I feel frustrated in specific situations. During these times, I examine both the facts of the situation and my attitude. Then, I decide where I want to go next and I start taking action toward that.

I have a daily meditation practice. Every day, as part of this practice I imagine I am living my ideal life. The things I might be doing, who is there with me, and what it feels like to be there.

By making a daily habit of focusing on what we want, and deciding on a plan to make it a reality, we gain clarity and are better able to see opportunities that arise around us. This also helps us make the day to day decisions that, over time lead us closer to our goals.

I really focus to make time in my day to work on projects and activities that steer me in the right direction. Some of these activities include building my next online course so I can better move toward the purpose in the work aspect of my life, making time to go for a run, and spending quality time with my family and friends. I put in the effort to make my ideal life, business, and business transition happen. Why? Because my ideal life isn't just going to fall into my lap and neither will yours. We have to work for it.

I keep on track by being patient and grateful. I am patient that I may not have all the answers, but I keep on going. When something goes wrong, I find it easier to shrug it off. I understand now that getting frustrated all the time about the small things will not help me get where I want to go.

I also find time in my regular meditations to pause and find three things to be grateful for that I have been working toward. They do not have to be profound and can be as simple as being grateful for family time together or the progress of one of my clients.

Your turn; think of one thing you are grateful for. Is it your family? A friend? A pet? A project you just completed? Working out yesterday? The leaves on a tree?

Think about what you are grateful for. Hold onto it. Now, picture it like it is right here with you. What did you notice or see? Did you notice your mood shift a bit? Taking a moment to be grateful holds some magic. It just takes a few seconds to tap into your gratitude and lift your mood! I think it's a superpower!

Remember, following this entire process takes some effort and repetition for stepping back to become a healthy habit.

Here are some other ideas you can bring into your daily life to help you further reinforce your own internal drive and accountability.

IDEA 1: FIND AN ACCOUNTABILITY PARTNER

Remember the Gail Matthews study? The one where she discussed how having a plan and following five simple steps can drastically increase your odds for success? Just in case you do not I have shared them again below:

1. Fully think through your goals
2. Write down your goals
3. Create action steps to make the goals happen
4. Share these goals and action steps with someone supportive
5. Create accountability by reporting back to them on a regular basis

We will cover a lot of these steps in the step back process but for additional support what can you do to bring more of steps 4 and 5 into your process?

Can you find someone to discuss the concepts, ideas and reflections in this book with and then set up times for each of you to share your goals, struggles and action items to move forward?

IDEA 2: WORK WITH A COACH

A good coach can be a game changer. I continue to work with some incredible coaches to help keep me on track, and this makes a huge difference. A good coach allows you to step back and do your own internal work to help you get past barriers, find steps to take, and better understand what is important to you. You can think of a coach as someone holding the rope as you scale the rock wall. You do the work while your coach creates a safe space where you are free to stretch your limits, and find that next handhold.

IDEA 3: STEP BACK SUNDAY

Designate a specific time of the week where you can go through your plan, check in and determine your next steps. On top of your regular weekly check-ins, I suggest choosing times throughout the year when you do a deeper dive into your plan—one where you can go through the four stages and do a compass check, and perhaps modify your map.

IDEA 4: REGULAR BUSINESS STRATEGY EXECUTION MEETINGS

If the plan you created is for your business or for your business transition, meet regularly with your team to help each other progress. Discuss challenges openly and create a meeting culture where people feel free to be open, honest, and growth-oriented. If you have employees but have not engaged them in your planning, think about doing so. If your goal is to reduce how much the business depends on you, what better way to help keep you on track?

IDEA 5: VISUALIZE YOUR IDEAL LIFE, BUSINESS OR TRANSITION ON A REGULAR BASIS

This is a key point! The more you think of what you want, the more your brain believes it to be possible. As a result, you'll start seeing the things that will help you move in the right direction.

• BONUS •

For a free video further explaining how you can incorporate the step back process into your day to day life visit **www.davesinclair.ca/numbbustingresources** now!

• STEP BACK REFLECTION •

In what ways might pressing pause and stepping back in your day to day life help you?

_____
_____
_____
_____
_____
_____
_____
_____
_____
_____

What would a day look like for you if you pressed pause and stepped back?

_____
_____
_____
_____
_____
_____
_____
_____
_____
_____
_____
_____

CHAPTER 12

Continuously Walking Through the Stages

Before we move into the second part of this book I want you to meet my client, Jerry. Jerry's story is a great example of how to use the four-stage step back process for life, business, and business transition. His story is one that shares how he used the four stages in every area of his life to stay grounded and get past those inevitable curveballs.

When Jerry and I started our journey together he owned a manufacturing and service business that was doing multi-million dollars in sales per year. From the outside, it appeared that Jerry had it made.

When he first started his business, it was small enough that he could be a part of it all and have a true relationship with each employee, as well as keep in direct contact with all the customers. He loved being able to connect to the people who helped him run the business, to meet the customers, and even get to know them beyond the buyer/seller relationship. This was and still remains a very important part of his identity.

Over the years, Jerry's company grew, branched out into new products, and as his employee base increased, his connection to it began to recede. With increasing growth, Jerry's passion dissolved because what he loved about running it was not there for him anymore. The business was running him and he started to feel depleted by it rather than energized as in the early years.

Jerry was disconnected, overworked, and grew numb as a result.

Meanwhile, even though on paper, he was doing great. Jerry had fallen out of love with it all. Sales were up, the company kept hiring, they retained their customer base and acquired new ones but Jerry's passion, desire, motivation, and connection were gone. He urgently wanted to get back on track with passion.

At this point, Jerry hired me as his business coach.

Jerry knew that for all to be okay, he had to overcome the numbness that had taken him over.

This is where we started.

During our first meeting together, Jerry said, "Dave, I've had enough of feeling this way. I think it would be best if I get out of the business. I just don't have the energy to get it to where I think it can go. Can you help me make this transition happen?"

At that moment, Jerry felt that his main goal was to sell the company, and that doing this would bring him to a better state of mind.

We started the process and below are a few of the different step backs that Jerry took. They demonstrate the power of continuing to use the process and how being grounded in your vision of what you truly want in life can help you persevere. Even when the world throws you a curveball.

STEP BACK 1: JERRY CONSIDERS SELLING HIS BUSINESS… OR WAS THERE MORE? (MONTH 0-3 AND ONGOING)

Where am I right now?

During our first meeting, Jerry said he wanted to sell the business. I asked when. He said "The sooner the better… within 6 months."

We talked about this and how a very well-prepared business may be able to sell in 6 months and how unprepared business could take 2-5 years to properly plan and complete a sale. With this in mind, we turned our attention to his business.

We did some quick initial evaluations of the business (starting with a lot of the tools you will get to use in the second half of this book). We also went deeper in the first couple of months and looked at what the business may be worth, who the best buyers may be for the business, and started to look to see if the sale of the business would provide the funds Jerry would need to live the next stage of his life. This is when things got really interesting.

Two things started to become quite clear to Jerry:

The business was not anywhere near where it needed to be to allow Jerry to retire and live off the proceeds of the sale.

Jerry was really quite uncertain about what he would do if he did not have the business in his life.

At this point, if you are a business owner, you may be connecting with Jerry here. Let me reassure you, you are not alone.

When looking to sell your business the financial picture is rarely the key challenge. Even if a business owner does get the money from the sale the bigger question is often, what would you do with your life afterward? What is it you want your life to be like as a result of selling the business?

So, Jerry and I went deeper…

I encouraged him to take a further step back by asking, 'Why sell the business?' My goal behind this question was to uncover what he really wanted. What would selling the business solve? When we take that first step back it is important to just ask yourself, what do you want?

As a result, Jerry began to closely examine his business and life. He could see he was not happy, but by going deeper he also realized he didn't know what would make him happy. To get toward his ideal life and business, he needed a plan before thinking about selling his business again.

Where do I want to go?

At this point in our work together, Jerry created a new vision for his life and relationships. In his new vision, he would reconnect with family and live a vibrant and exciting life. He also outlined that he would become involved in his family's lives by making himself more available to them.

Through this process that I took him through, Jerry was able to see that his devotion to his business could cost him dearly if he was to let it go further. It had the risk of pulling him away from his family. His vision included a re-dedication to his family. As part of creating his new vision for his life, Jerry pictured a time where he could be an even bigger part of his future grandchildren's lives as well. He also envisioned what he would feel like when he was living a more healthy lifestyle, spending more time on hobbies, and having the freedom to travel more.

Jerry still wanted to be involved in business but he needed it to be manageable and meaningful. He knew for sure that big business was not for him.

How do I get there?

The first step Jerry took was to keep reminding himself of what he wanted and to schedule time for this into his calendar. The next thing he did was to pick up books that would help him move toward living his ideal life. Both these steps held him accountable and motivated to keep moving toward his ideal life as laid out in his plan.

The results started to come and he started to have more of what he said he wanted.

How do I stay on track?

Once Jerry was living his values he saw that every day things started to change. His life was transforming slowly over time, step by step. Patience was his ally and gratitude reminded him to stay on track as he reconnected with all that really mattered to him.

> **STEP BACK 2: HOW DO I CREATE A BUSINESS THAT SUPPORTS MY IDEAL LIFE? (MONTH 3 TO YEAR 4)**

Where am I now?

The second step back question Jerry worked on was: "How do I create a business that supports my ideal life, and that can ultimately be transitioned to new owners while still giving me a financial reward?"

The answer Jerry came up with helped to formulate a plan. In order for Jerry to fully answer this question, he needed to look at every aspect of his business from every angle to determine what needed to be changed or fixed before it got sold.

Jerry's business got to a point where it relied too heavily on him. If Jerry wanted to end up with a business that allowed him the time to live his ideal life and have a business that would be more attractive to outside investors, he would need to put structures in place so the work would not rely solely on him.

Where do I want to go?

Jerry went on to create a vision of his business that would allow him to have his ideal life. He could see the business not really needing him to be there, and he would only commit to work that inspired him. He envisioned a company with loyal employees and a strong process for sales that would enable him to take a month-long vacation every year.

If he could get to this point then it would fill him with passion again and would make it easier to sell. Jerry also realized that if this could happen and if it was aligned with his vision, he might not even sell. Jerry was starting to find some much-needed passion for his business again.

How do I get there?

Mainly, Jerry's plan was focused on reducing the reliance of the business on him. It included engaging his team to create a shared vision, defining values, and mentoring key staff. It also included ensuring that the passion and purpose Jerry was feeling would be transferred to everyone else in the company. This created a company culture that was also aligned with his ideal business plan.

How do I stay on track?

With regard to the business, Jerry started to work on the plan he put in place and was starting to see some real progress.

We touched base regularly, which allowed Jerry to maintain awareness of his goals and to keep up with the right work to support his ideal business vision, and ideal life.

> **STEP BACK 3: JERRY'S WORLD TAKES A TURN (YEAR 4-5)**

Where am I now?

He put a plan in place for his ideal life and ideal business that excited him, and things were slowly moving forward. Sales were up, although things were not perfect Jerry could still see the light at the end of the tunnel.

Then there was an economic downturn. The industry itself started to change significantly and the final straw came when Jerry discovered one of his key employees had been falsifying financial records. It all quickly became unraveled. Jerry had to take another step back to examine the situation with these new circumstances.

We mapped out his options and Jerry realized he had to make a tough choice. He'd either revisit his transition out of the business or shut it down. After many step backs and a little agonizing over it, Jerry made the decision to sell.

Where do I want to go?

With this new understanding that the business was not everything, and knowing that it was time to leave, Jerry put together a vision of the potential transition with a worst-case (liquidation of all assets) and a best-case scenario (selling the company for a decent price to an outside investor). This vision allowed Jerry to prepare for the worst while continuing to aim for the best case.

How do I get there?

Jerry remained focused on what *could be* rather than falling victim to going numb and giving up.

With my help, he outlined a plan to discover financially-viable options and to reach out to buyers who had previously expressed interest. By sticking to his plan and by persevering, Jerry identified a few options, and in the end, was able to get out of his business without suffering a large loss.

Since Jerry had both the plan for his ideal life, and the bones of the transition plan in place, he was better positioned to talk to the potential buyers as well as his accountants, to work with everyone and come up with a deal that made the most sense. Jerry was entrepreneurial and was able to negotiate to hold onto the most profitable part of the business. The most profitable part of his business was the part he originally built. It was small and just what he wanted. Again, something that was in true alignment with what Jerry really wanted from life.

How do I stay on track?

For Jerry's business transition, although it certainly wasn't easy, he remained open to the process and possibilities that were happening during each moment. A key step that helped Jerry stay on track is when he called a family meeting (remember his re-dedication to his family in his initial vision) and let them know what was going on. This allowed Jerry to go from feeling he was in this alone to having the support and understanding of what was most important to him, his family.

This openness allowed him to remain centered, strong, and patient. He did the tough work and learned new skills along the way. When questions came up he took the steps to find answers.

STEP BACK 4: BEYOND THE TRANSITION (YEAR 5 AND BEYOND!)

Where am I now?

The transition went by, the dust settled and Jerry stepped back again. He was grateful to realize that he was actually in a good position and he could see new ways to grow and learn in his new ideal life.

Where do I want to go?

With a vision in place that he's comfortable with, Jerry can see how he has grown and expanded. His new vision is fluid and dynamic and includes what feels aligned with who he is today and where he is at.

Jerry sees himself running a smaller version of the original business. He sees himself working with volunteer organizations, standing up for causes that are important to him. He sees himself reading and continuing to learn while also taking care of his overall well-being and working on deepening his relationships with his family and new grandchildren.

As I listened to Jerry share this new vision with me, I could see his body settle as he relaxed into it. This vision is who he is.

How do I get there?

With all that Jerry had gone through to get to this point, he was now able to further tap into what was truly important to him. Jerry's current plan allows him the freedom to go after what inspires him as well as enough structure to keep him focused on what he knows will keep him healthy in body and soul.

How do I stay on track?

We still talk and work together regularly. Jerry has a new lens and new tools to ensure his journey continues.

After having gone through this coaching process with me, Jerry had a vision for his ideal life and business. He had a plan to realize his vision and he followed through. Jerry learned a lot about himself and was able to overcome twists and turns (including a major economic downturn). Regular check-in calls with me, as his coach helped him stay grounded in all of this.

While working with Jerry I got to see him define his own version of success and witness him stay true to it.

With every client, just knowing that they allow me into their transformation process and trust me with this part of their journey through business, life, and relationships is not something I ever take for granted. It is an honor and a privilege that leads my work – the clients I work with and me – feeling that I am their teammate, coach, and friend.

• STEP BACK REFLECTION •

Thank you for taking the time to read the first half of this book. What new insights or key points have come up for you?

PART TWO
Moving Forward by Stepping Back!

In the first half of this book, I outlined stepping back as a concept. Now I want to introduce a more practical perspective that will allow you to start using it right now.

In the next three chapters, you'll put the step back process to work in three major areas of concern to all business owners: the ideal life, business, and transition. It is time to put concept into action!!!

> If you are reading the ebook version or are not a fan of writing in books, no worries! You can download a companion workbook on my website at **www.davesinclair.ca/numbbustingresources** or purchase a paperback workbook/journal version on Amazon.

"You only have control over three things in your life – the thoughts you think, the images you visualize, and the actions you take."

JACK CANFIELD, author, motivational speaker, corporate trainer, and entrepreneur

We tend to make things harder and more complicated than they really are. Instead of trying to control everything that happens in life, we are more effective when we break things down into their simplest form, as Canfield suggests.

If you want to create change, remember there are really only four things you need to look at:

Based on what you have learned so far, I now invite you to take a moment to reflect on your life, your business, or your business transition. Try not to overthink your answers at this point as you will have a chance to dive deeper in the next few chapters. Just take a few moments here and jot down what comes up for you as you think through the four key questions on the next page.

Where are you now?
___
___
___
___

Where do you want to go?
___
___
___
___

How will you get there?
___
___
___
___

How will you keep yourself on track?
___
___
___
___

I want to help you see how quickly and easily you can begin turning the ship in the right direction. It is common to get lost in the planning process to the point where it eats up all your time and energy. Using my process can help you make strong progress toward the changes you want in a short period of time while still feeling energized.

In the chapters ahead, I'll illustrate how these questions can be modified to fit three specific situations: your life, a business and a business transition. Beyond these, feel free to use the step back process with any change or transition.

> Don't forget that you can download a companion workbook on my website at
> www.davesinclair.ca/numbbustingresources

CHAPTER 13
The Art and Science of Creating Your Ideal Life

It's time to put the step back process into practice. Are you ready to start taking action toward forming your ideal life?

STAGE 1: WHERE ARE YOU NOW?

Change is far easier to accomplish if you believe that it's possible. To see where you currently sit in terms of a growth mindset, take this short quiz.

Rank each question from 1-5, with 1 being completely false and 5 always true. (1 = completely false, 2 = mostly false, 3 = in the middle 4 = mostly true, 5 = always true)

TAKE THE GROWTH MINDSET QUIZ

Worksheet 13.1

STATEMENT	YOUR SCORE
You can change your intelligence over time	
You can change the type of person you are	
You can change aspects of your basic personality	
You can learn and develop new skills	
Effort is a key determinant of success	
Learning new things can be enjoyable	
Talent can be learned	
The more you deliberately practice something, the better you will perform	
Total score:	
TOTAL POSSIBLE SCORE:	**40**

The higher your score, the more you believe in the concept that you can learn and grow. Do you believe you can develop the skills, build new talents, and increase intelligence through practice and effort? It is amazing, and although it takes time, I can attest to the fact that dedicated effort and practice has showered me with opportunities that I never imagined possible.

I can honestly say that at age 49, I am more physically and mentally alive than at any other point in my life. I attribute this to the fact that I know I can continue to learn and grow.

I also know I have to give up trying to be perfect and accept being OK with not getting it right the first time. Perfect can be the enemy of growth if we keep thinking about how far away it is and that we will never be as good as someone else at something.

Instead of seeking perfection, pursue mastery.

Ask yourself: What do I need to do to become just a little better at this than yesterday? And be OK with failing at something. It may take a lot of work and a lot of missteps before you get there, but just think of what you will learn and how you will grow along the way.

Worksheet 13.2

What did you notice after you took the growth mindset quiz and read this section? What are your ideas for developing more of a growth mindset?

> **• BONUS •**
>
> For a free video further explaining growth mindset and how you can bring more of this into your life visit **www.davesinclair.ca/numbbustingresources** now!

Now that you have a plan for developing a growth mindset, let's take a little closer look at where you are. If you don't have all the answers, don't stress. Just come back to this when you can. The whole process is meant to be the opposite of stressful. It is meant to be uplifting and enlightening.

Remember to take mini breaks by inhaling through your nose, and fully exhaling out through your mouth. It's amazing what just a couple of slow deep breaths in and out can do for your overall state of mind.

Next it is time to take a look at what is going on in your mind and the story about where you are right now.

As you consider the questions that I've previously outlined in chapter 7, I invite you to answer these same questions. Reflect on them and respond in the way that best fits you, whether it's taking notes or drawing a picture or using the separate companion workbook.

I share an example from my own journey of transformation to demonstrate how I feel I would have answered these questions in the early days of my path forward. Hopefully this helps you see that none of us are alone.

Worksheet 13.3

Can you describe, as objectively as possible the way you are living your life right now? What are the facts a reporter would observe?

My answer:

I found myself at the point where I had gotten drunk, caused a disturbance and was taken to a detention cell to sleep it off. I had been drinking more and more, found myself spending less time with my family and had recently left a business that I had helped grow over the last 20 years. I was 70 pounds overweight, did not exercise a lot, and had few friends, no hobbies, and was not in touch with my spiritual side. I didn't have a good sense of about what the future held. I wanted to change but was unsure how to do this and felt unsure, alone and numb.

Your answer:

NUMB?

What is it that you may be telling yourself about your life right now? What is the internal voice in your head saying to you?

My answer:

> *My inner voice tells me: Oh, crap. Now what have I done? How am I going to recover from this? What does my wife think? How about the kids? How about everyone else? How am I ever going to face people? I need to get out of here and take off! It's hopeless, and I am going to be unhappy forever!*

Your answer:

> *Do you really believe everything your internal voice is saying? Do the facts of the story match what it is that you are saying? If you were talking to a true friend in the same situation how would you speak to them? What advice might you offer?*

My answer:

> So things are a little harsh right now. What if being in jail is just the wake-up you need to move forward? It's not hopeless, people can change. You can change. You can show yourself and others what a new Dave can look like. What might be the first thing you can do to step forward? You can do this; I believe in you.

Your answer:

> **What is it you may want to change internally, embrace, or let go of so you can take the next steps in creating your ideal life?**

My answer:

> *Enough is enough. I've been thinking there is some smoke here for some time, and now it's a fire. It's time to change, and the first step is to give up drinking. You don't need it in your life, and it's holding you back. You can do this! You can get this monkey off your back, and it's time for you to own it!*

As I started down the path of change, my answer also changed:

> *I've given up the drinking. Great work! To make it stick I think there may be some other things I need to give up. It's time to give up the loneliness I felt when I was younger. Give up thinking I was wronged here, and that I missed out on so much, and instead see this time as a gift that shows me how much I now treasure connection. I am good enough. I'm worthy of connection, love, and peace.*

As you can see, you start with the external shift you want to make and, as time goes on, you start to see some more important internal shifts that need to happen. It's a progression, and that is why this process is so powerful when you repeat it. Start where you can and be gentle with yourself.

Your answer:

Congratulations! By answering these questions, you've begun the process. What are you noticing already? This stage in and of itself is already a huge first step! You looked at where you are now, and perhaps you even have an idea about some of the shifts—internal and external—you may need to make moving forward.

STAGE 2: YOUR DESTINATION

This is the part where you say what you really want. It's another step back in a series of ongoing moments you need to give yourself to have your dream life. The problem isn't wanting it all. The problem is not knowing what your ALL is!

Make sure you've got a little time to yourself and follow along as I give you the quick-start way to gain clarity about yourself and your life.

Imagine yourself being fully immersed in living your ideal life. By ideal, I mean a life where you feel completely alive and fulfilled, living true to what is most important to you. Sink into the experience, as if you are really there. What are you noticing about your ideal life? Do you hear anything? See anything? Smell or feel anything?

Who is there with you? What are you doing as you start your day? What are you doing the next day? How about the next week? What is going on in your life that is filling you up and bringing you such contentment and pleasure? What is there beyond the money you have acquired, the things you have in your life, and what you do for work?

If you find you're having trouble envisioning this scenario, don't stress about it. You might be trying too hard. Just take a couple of deep breaths and trust yourself to get a glimpse of what I promise is somewhere inside, waiting for you to notice.

Stay lost in that feeling of having your ALL for as long as you want, then consider your answers to the next questions.

Worksheet 13.4

What is coming up for you? What are you starting to notice could be in your ideal life?

These feelings around your ideal life will become your **guiding compass**, and I am going to show you how to experience it more, all the time.

Does it all feel a bit overwhelming? Are you still feeling a bit stuck? I know I did when I started.

When I started my journey back in 2012, well before I had anything figured out, I still stepped into the process above. I remember the moment someone asked, "Dave, what is it that you most fully want in your life?"

It hit me almost instantly. I wanted inner peace and love.

Next, they asked me what life would look like with more inner peace and love—what I would be doing and who would be there with me. They allowed me the time to experience this as if I had it all right now. It was powerful, to say the least.

I can see how this simple answer helped guide me to the vision I have for my life now and toward the process I developed to help kickstart you toward finding your own vision.

In the end, if a simple question such as, "What is it that you most fully want in life?" helps you, go with it. Even if it is one word, sink into that word or that feeling, and then read on.

Take some time now and capture what is coming up for you so far.

• BONUS: IDEAL LIFE VISUALIZATION •

For a free guided visualization exercise that can take you deeper into this experience and the process ahead download the "Ideal Life Visualization" at **http://davesinclair.ca/numbbustingresources**

NUMB?

Worksheet 13.5

What is coming up for you? Are there any core themes or core ideas you would like to see show up in your ideal life? What core feelings would you like to have in your ideal life?

One of the most compelling reasons to regularly take a STEP BACK to envision your ideal life is to return to that feeling. Teaching yourself to live with that feeling each day takes time and conscious effort, but could there be anything more worth it?

No! We all want to feel good about our lives but feeling good living our lives is what we're really after.

Living the life of your dreams is both an art and a science. So let's take what you've envisioned and make it a little more tangible.

What different things did you see yourself doing or experiencing in your life? It is the fulfillment of these different parts of us that creates an ideal life.

Here are some areas of life that are common to many people, but I also invite you to keep your list true to what matters to you. Use words that resonate for you, too.

- Career/job/business...
- Career development
- Personal time
- Recreation
- Travel
- Friends
- Family
- Social life
- Health
- Wellness
- Mental well-being
- Community
- Volunteer time
- Financial
- Spiritual
- Where we live
- Spouse/partner
- Personal development

What other aspects are right for you?

I invite you to write down 6-10 key areas of life that when running smoothly lead you to living your ideal life.

Worksheet 13.6

THE KEY ASPECTS OF YOUR IDEAL LIFE		

In a moment, we'll start working with your list, so take time to review and tweak it, if necessary.

You don't have to get it perfect. (There is no such thing!) Just do your best, knowing it will evolve over time, because **you** will evolve over time. That's why I encourage you to come back to this point often and revisit this work!

Now that you know your different life aspects, divide the blank circle on the next page into equal segments. Once you have divided your circle, write one aspect in each piece of the pie.

To help you get started, the image below is an example of my life aspects.

MY KEY LIFE ASPECTS

- Where We Live
- My Work
- Giving Back
- Financial Security
- Gaylene
- Recreation
- Growth
- Family and Friends
- Spirituality
- Health

Note: You will come back to this page later on in the chapter as well to create your mini visions for each of these aspects!

Worksheet 13.7

YOUR IDEAL LIFE

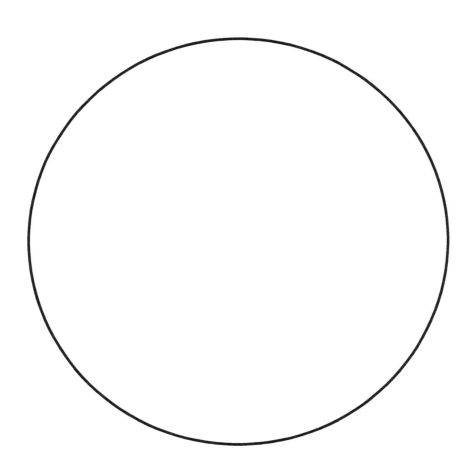

Bravo! You've just started a visual outline of where you want to go! Now, let's get you back to the feeling of being at an ideal state in each aspect to help bring this outline to life.

In addition to naming each aspect of your Ideal Life, you're going to add two things about each one in Worksheet 13.8. It does not need to be much. A few words or a sentence is a great start. It could even be an image if that is what works for you!

- **WHAT** you want. Describe how you want to feel in this aspect of your ideal life.
- **WHY** it matters to you. Why is what you want and having yourself showing up this way in your life important to you?

Once you have completed Worksheet 13.8, I invite you to go back to your wheel above and add a few words to each aspect of your ideal life vision. Adding a few new words will help you create mini visions of how you want your life to be and feel like in each of your different life aspects. Worksheet 13.9 can help you come up with these mini vision statements.

Use the work you did before to come up with a statement that fits in each aspect. All that matters here is that the declaration you came up with for each aspect feels right for you. Each one of your aspects should provide you with a sense of direction in how you want to show up when you are living your ideal life.

Worksheet 13.8

LIFE ASPECT	WHAT YOU WANT	WHY IT MATTERS
My example: Health	I am happy, healthy, and having fun. I am around 200 lbs. and able to run a half marathon whenever I want to.	I want to be in control of my mind, body, and spirit. A strong body is a foundation for the rest.

THE ART AND SCIENCE OF CREATING YOUR IDEAL LIFE

NUMB?

Worksheet 13.9

LIFE ASPECT	MINI VISION FOR THIS ASPECT (WHAT DO YOU WANT THIS TO BE LIKE AND WHY?)

THE ART AND SCIENCE OF CREATING YOUR IDEAL LIFE

The visual you create is meant to be something you can come back to that allows you to tap into the feeling you get as you envision your ideal life. This is an important step, and I encourage you to take a few moments to do this. The act of writing this may provide further clarity in terms of what you want to shift in your life.

For reference, please see the current draft of my life vision and how I combined the what and why statements for each life aspect. I like to have everything in one spot. I also love pie charts and have this ideal life vision in a few strategic spots so I can refer to it often. *NOTE: If you can, make a couple of copies of your completed wheel so you can use it for the next steps!*

MY DEFINITION OF SUCCESS

- **Where we live-** We are living in a nice house with a built in greenhouse. We overlook a wonderful spot in nature, and are able to exercise outside all year, We are close to town, yet have the privacy we need to connect with nature.
- **My work-** My mission is to help individuals and organizations first define what success is to them and to empower them to create their own road map to achieve this. This work feeds my soul, provides abundant security, while I work 16-24 hours per week
- **Giving Back-** I continue to mentor, guide, and coach people meeting them where they are. I facilitate a men's group to aid those faced with varying forms of addiction.
- **Financial Security-** I can look at our investments, savings, and bank account and know our financial future is well taken care of
- **Gaylene-** Love. Harmony. Teamwork. Passion. My soulmate. Our own lives as individuals together. We are bulletproof
- **Recreation-** We are taking a few of trips per year and have fulfilling hobbies
- **Growth-** I am taking in the small moments allowing them to further develop my positive mental foundation. I read, learn, and share topics that are of interest to me and that can further support mankind.
- **Family and Friends-** I am connecting and spending time with people I love, and they love me. This provides a deep feeling of human connection.
- **Spirituality-** I am continually awakening to the future that I am a part of. I do this through the small wonders in the world that I can learn from. Patience is my guide, fulfilled balance is my goal, and mindfulness is my path.
- **Health-** I am happy, healthy and having fun. I am around 200#s and able to run a half marathon whenever I want to, I am an inspiration to others.

How are you making out? Are you gaining clarity on what is really important to you? Are you starting to see the key ideas and qualities that could lead to you living your best life if you consistently followed them?

What I'm really asking you here is; what are the core values that you hold important in living your life? If you're not clear and still want to explore this, take a look at the column "Why it matters." I suspect some of your values live there.

Take some time to see what values come up for you and jot them down. What words feel right? Which ones come alive for you? Again, it doesn't have to be perfect right now. This is just a start, and I welcome you to come back to this often as you continue to learn and grow.

Knowing what really matters to you will help you make better decisions and guide your behavior. The result is you living a more well-aligned life every day—one filled with passion arising from what is deeply important to you.

Worksheet 13.10

I am noticing these value words:

To tap even deeper into your values, here is another exercise that always gets results with my clients.

Imagine you are at a party held in your honor sometime in the future. You have aged well and are filled with all kinds of wonderful memories of a life well lived. People have shared story after story about you.

It has been a very full day, and there is a break in the festivities. At this point, two of your grandchildren (or if this is not in your cards for an ideal life, simply substitute the word grandchildren for two young people) come up to you to chat. They are fascinated by the life you've lived and ask you for advice.

What three pieces of advice would you provide? If you have more than three, that's great. They are all ears!

In the worksheet on the following page first jot down your advice in the second column. Once you have done this, take a step back and ask yourself: What value or values, that is/are true to me, does this advice represent? Add this value word/phrase or words and phrases to the value column. You have likely just touched upon a key value of yours and a definition on how to live it! How can this help you moving forward?

Worksheet 13.11

VALUE WORD	WHAT ADVICE WOULD YOU GIVE OTHERS BASED ON THIS WORD?

How would the advice you give others affect you if you were to follow it now? In what ways might you be able to incorporate this advice into your daily life?

The list you have come up with may not be a complete list of your values, and can be added to over time. Does it feel like a good start to you though? Nice work. I know it took me time but it was work worth doing!

I now have a list of values and what they mean to me that I go over during my morning meditations. I also find myself reciting this list to myself when things get a bit challenging. By doing these two things, I am better equipped to make decisions in the present that are aligned with my values and what I really want in life.

How about you? In what ways can you commit to incorporating your values into your life moving forward, and what can happen if you do this?

Worksheet 13.12

How can I incorporate my values even more into my life?

> It's not hard to make decisions when you know what your values are.
>
> ROY E. DISNEY

What you've just done is laying the foundation for defining your ideal life **vision**, **purpose**, and **values**. Over time, you can come back to this foundation to further refine your vision, purpose, and values if you feel it is required.

For now, take a couple of deep breaths and feel grateful for the work you have stepped back to do. You've already accomplished some very meaningful work.

STAGE 3: HOW WILL YOU GET THERE?

Say you have a choice between watching an extra hour of TV or going for a walk with your partner. Pause for a moment and bring the vision of your ideal life front and center in your mind. Now, mentally run through your values. How does this impact your decision?

Should you decide to choose the walk – perhaps honoring the family and health values that are important to you – how does it feel while you are walking, and after the walk? Do you feel accomplished and fulfilled? Does it feel you are moving in the right direction? By adopting this idea of choosing what is aligned with your values and vision, what could your life look like in say one week? How about one month? One year? How about after making decisions in your daily life for 10 years? Where could this lead you?

How might you adopt this practice into your lifestyle for the many decisions that you face each day?

NUMB?

> Orient yourself properly. Then and only then concentrate on the day.
> Set your sights at the Good, the Beautiful, and the True, and then focus pointedly and carefully on the concerns of each moment.
>
> JORDAN PETERSON,
> Canadian clinical psychologist and author of 12 RULES FOR LIFE

And now, you might be wondering; how about some of the bigger changes you want to tackle that have you feeling a bit stuck?

Perhaps you know the change you want to make, but don't know how the heck to do it. Many people start to feel overwhelmed at this point. An ideal life can seem far away, and they begin to ask themselves how they will ever achieve it. This is why many people never make changes. They dream of an ideal life, but don't act. That's where this stage of the process lends a hand.

And this stage is more fun than you might think. It might feel as if you're light years away from your ideal life, but I urge you to dive in and see if that's really true.

Here's how you'll do it:

How are you doing in terms of where you are right now compared to where you want to go?

Divide the circle in worksheet 13.13 into how many life aspects you have. Next, write the name of your key aspects into the different segments.

Think about where you are for each part on a scale of 1-10 versus where you would like to be. 1 represents "not at all where I want to be" and 10 is "This part of my life is exactly how I want to have it."

If there's a category where you're really knocking it out of the park, color in that complete segment, from the center to the outer edge.

If you're only half-way there, color it in half-way from the center, out.

If you're barely making a dent in that category, just color a little bit from the center, out.

Go ahead and begin coloring your pie in **as it makes sense right now!**

Use my pie chart as an example, looking at how I rank the different aspects of my life at this point in time.

Here is an example of what my pie chart looks like now:

HOW AM I STACKING UP TO MY DEFINITION OF SUCCESS TODAY?

Categories: Where We Live, My Work, Financial Security, Recreation, Family and Friends, Health, Spirituality, Growth, Gaylene, Giving Back

NUMB?

Worksheet 13.13

CURRENT RANKING OF YOUR IDEAL LIFE

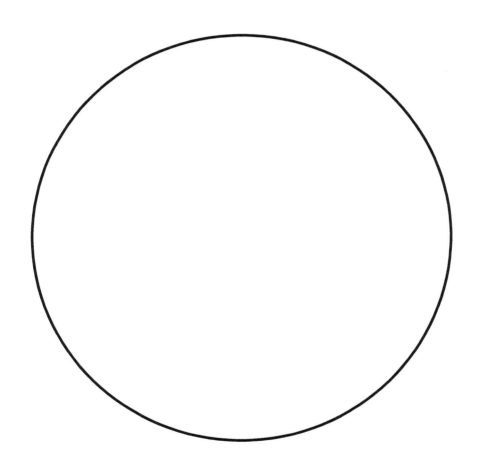

When you're done, take some time to absorb what your pie is telling you. Look at how it is shaded and see what insight it provides you.

Part of the reason people shut down about doing this work is they think they'll have to take on everything at once.

That is not the case at all.

The next exercise coming up is here to make things feel more manageable. Whenever I am feeling a bit overwhelmed, I come back to this step.

By stepping back to do this simple exercise, you can see which gears in the complex systems we call "our lives" might need a bit of maintenance for the rest of the system to run smoother.

Look at the story your pie chart tells you. How satisfied are you with your pie chart right now? What is going well? What might need a bit of maintenance so your wheel can spin more freely?

Continuing with my example, what I found was that overall I was very satisfied with most of the aspects of my life. I did get the strong feeling that I wanted to focus a bit more energy on family and friends. You see I can easily pull back inside myself quite often (especially when I am working on a big project like writing this book) and forget the great feelings I get when I have a strong support network in place. In short, I miss the feeling of the human connection.

I also realized that although it would take time to keep in touch with the ones I love, the energy I would gain from doing this would easily spill into other aspects of my life.

NUMB?

Worksheet 13.14

What story is the pie chart of your life telling you? What is going well? What could use some attention? Which one or two aspects could you focus on that would have the most impact on your life and vision as a whole?

Ok, so now what?

You know what you want, and you have selected a couple of key aspects in your life that you want to put your attention to. These projects can still feel a bit overwhelming. Now it's time to get more specific and break them down into even smaller pieces.

What are some small initiatives (life aspect improvement projects) that will increase your level of satisfaction with one aspect of your life, or your life overall? A few examples could be starting a running program, learning a new language, creating a family event, etc.

What key things in that segment could you work on to move toward your ideal life vision?

For me, some initiatives that come to mind are: organize a regular family retreat, join an exercise group, and join a reading group, among others.

Take a minute to answer this question for yourself.

Worksheet 13.15

What are some potential initiatives that could lead to the mini visions you have for your different life aspects?

If you feel like there are too many initiatives to tackle at once, you are probably right. It is still good to write down whatever comes to mind.

Remember that less is more when it comes to change. You can always come back to this list later in the process.

Now comes the fun part. Select one initiative for now. That's all—just one that you feel works best right now and will have the biggest overall impact.

Worksheet 13.16

> *Take a moment and select one initiative. What is it?*

Let's help you break this into bite-sized chunks.

Remember when I talked about eating that elephant? Well, it's time to start eating by breaking the initiative down into very small steps. Once you know the steps, decide what you'll do first. If you are recruiting help, who will do what? Lay it all out like a mini-plan and start acting on it.

Fill out the tracking template on the following page with a few action steps you will take to get a solid start on this important initiative. I provide an example with my plan to increase my connection to family and friends, as well as a blank plan for you.

As you will notice, there's one more section that I haven't yet mentioned, and it's about the benefits of this initiative. In this section, step back again and think of how changing this one piece will positively impact your overall life. Thinking about this impact will increase your desire to do the work ahead.

DAVE'S SAMPLE INITIATIVE

Worksheet 13.17

Initiative: Organize an initial family retreat weekend at a destination where there is a run/walk that has meaning for us as a family.	What are the benefits of this initiative? Increased connection with family, improve health, contribute to a worthy cause, lead to this being an annual event to further build connection.	
Tasks (action steps)	Who will do this?	When will this be done?
Follow up with family members who said they were interested earlier this year and see if people are still interested.	Dave	Done
Find most central spot to do the event.	Dave	Oct 24
Find list of events/fairs/causes in a central location.	Dave	Oct 31
Create a survey to send to family with your lists and different locations, events, and where to stay (camping, hotels, etc.).	Dave	Nov 7
Send out survey, gather responses, select the most popular event, etc.	Dave	Nov 14
Send booking info out to everyone	Dave	Dec 7
Enjoy the weekend!	Dave	TBD

Initiative:	What are the benefits of this initiative?	
Tasks (action steps)	Who will do this?	When will this be done?

The point here is to break things down into actionable steps with deadlines you can commit to.

After the first initiative is done, repeat the process and keep making progress in whichever aspect makes sense next.

It's important to note that you do not have to completely improve one aspect before working on another aspect of your life. Remember, it's a system. What needs the most attention right now? Try to focus on that. When it feels like it's moving in the right direction, step back again to see what else needs attention.

STAGE 4: PATIENCE & GRATITUDE – HOW DO YOU STAY ON TRACK?

To start this stage, I invite you to step back for a moment and ask yourself how important having your ideal life is to you. What would it provide you? Imagine how you would feel if you were able to step fully into this life right now? What do you notice?

For me, success is defined by constantly moving toward my ideal life. I spent much of my time chasing material things and trying to impress people with the work Me. It was not making me happy. I knew there was more and I wanted more. I want it all. And I now have a pretty great idea of what that can look like. It looks like a smile on my face and it feels like passion, purpose and creation.

Worksheet 13.18

> **Why is having an ideal life important to you? What would this ideal life provide to you personally? How would it feel to be making progress toward this ideal life?**

Taking the time to regularly come back to the feeling of your ideal life is a powerful way to help you keep on track.

Now that you know what is important to you in your life, and why it is important, I invite you to do the following exercise. If you can carve out **5-10 minutes to repeat this every day**, that would be great. You may want to have your ideal life vision you have created in this chapter with you until you commit it to memory.

If you can't do this daily, I invite you to start out by doing this just once a week or when you remember. I'm sure you will start to see the benefits. To help build this habit, print out your completed vision and place it somewhere as a reminder.

Even if you only have a few aspects of your life vision wheel completed in stage 2, this is still a great time to start this exercise. It'll help you see what else comes up so you can fill in more areas. I've found that by doing this, I have modified and enriched my life vision over time. The practice allows me a chance to reflect on what I really want daily and to act toward it.

Start by taking a moment (I do this early in the morning) to sit and relax. Focus on your breathing. Take a few deep breaths in through your nose, and out through your mouth. Settle into the spot where you're sitting and focus on your breath.

Imagine yourself living your ideal life right now. Living in the ways that you have captured on your life wheel. What do you see, smell, hear, feel? Who is here with you? What do you do as you start your day all the way through till you are going to sleep? What do you notice? Take the time you deserve and pay attention to what you notice as you are here. Once you have experienced your ideal life, bring your attention back to your body and your room, open your eyes if they were closed, and rest for a second.

Doing this visualization on a regular basis, as I do each morning, will lead you closer and closer to what you want in life. The exercise, if done enough, can also rewire your brain to allow you to see that what you are visualizing is possible! Believing it is possible provides the fuel you need to make changes and lead you toward making small choices throughout your day. Those small choices will then naturally lead you toward your ideal life! Combining this visualization by completing your action steps above will help you move closer to your ideal life.

Be grateful

Two more things that will help you keep on track are gratitude and patience.

For gratitude, I like to keep the exercises simple. The important thing with the below exercise is to pick a time of day and stick with it. It may seem like a bit of work at first but repetition builds habit. And of all the habits I have, taking the time to be grateful is one of the most fulfilling and enriching.

The Gratitude Exercise:

- Take a few moments to be still.
- Take a few deep breaths in and out and, once you are ready, ask yourself:
- What three things am I grateful for in my life right now? Take a moment to think about how it feels to have those things in your life.
- What actions from yesterday am I grateful for that are helping me move toward my ideal life? Take a moment and really feel the progress and be grateful to yourself for taking the steps!

That's it!

Were you grateful for a warm day or a loving family? The more specific you are, the better. And when you are grateful, truly sink into that feeling. You may find yourself smiling just a little more.

If you can't find something to be grateful for in the moment, be grateful you are taking the time to think of something you can do today so you can be grateful tomorrow.

To enhance this exercise, keep a journal. The act of writing helps to cement these feelings of gratitude in your mind. It is amazing what happens as you start this daily practice. You may even find you start walking around this world with more gratitude for everyone, including yourself!

> To download a guided meditation on the above exercise as well as a gratitude journal template, please visit
> **www.davesinclair.ca/numbbustingresources**

Be patient

The power of patience is amazing.

I frequently talk to clients and friends about patience and the results it can give us. If you compared what happens when someone tries to force progress versus when you allow progress to come through hard work, which one gives you the better results?

The latter requires patience. By no means am I saying it will not take work to bring your vision to life. Rather what I am trying to impress on you here is to be gentle on yourself as you do the work. Take a few small steps and see what happens. Step back regularly to see what is being provided to you after those steps. Allow yourself to learn. To grow. To figure out what you are all about.

It's like when I am training for a marathon. If I take longer to prepare and take care of myself along the way, chances are I will enjoy the training and the race itself a lot more. If I try to jam too much in too quickly, I will probably resent the training, the race will be less fun, and I may even injure myself.

Patience is the antidote to this. Take action, but also enjoy the process.

Getting in touch with what your ideal life can look and feel like, building gratitude, and being patient are critical to sustaining momentum as you create your ideal life. In addition, I cannot stress how important it is to repeat all the stages in this process. Finding a regular time to do this can help.

STEP BACK SUNDAY

Pick a day when you aren't normally overwhelmed with demands and do a weekly check-in with your vision, your plan, your emotions, and with the fire in your belly to achieve your ideal life. Go through the four key questions, and check in with where you are, where you are going, how you will get there, and how you can keep yourself on track. Literally blocking out this time in your calendar is a powerful way to help keep yourself on track.

This is also a great time to check in with your coach or accountability partner if you have one.

Sundays might be the best day to review your status, or perhaps another day works better for you. Just put something on your calendar to repeat every week at the same time. The importance of repetition—from examining your vision to checking in with your partner—cannot be overstated.

Repetition trains your mind.

Now choose how much time you can realistically give to this stage in the process. Fifteen minutes? Thirty minutes? An hour? It's your call.

What might seem like another to-do will actually become time during each week that feels more like a reward. **Stepping back** is the greatest gift we can give ourselves. We need time to reflect, renew and plan.

That's all this step needs to be. Make it yours.

One last thing: Remember the study on the power of setting a goal, writing it down, defining action steps, sharing it with someone, and then checking in regularly? Remember how doing these things dramatically increased the odds of completing projects?

If I could make a suggestion, it would be to pick a person in your life (or hire a coach) with whom to share your life dreams. It could be your spouse, a friend, or someone you think of as a peer or mentor. Pick your person carefully, because they need to offer you the right mix of unconditional support and honest feedback to help you stay accountable.

Their role will not be to judge you, but to ask helpful questions. They are there to help you stay engaged with your process, learn from things that don't go as planned, and understand how you might change things going forward.

This step has a two-fold purpose.

One is, we're all really good at procrastinating, avoiding our inner bully or thinking we're too busy to do this work. It helps to have someone we meet with regularly to keep us accountable.

We also all need a cheerleader who's in our court, rooting for our success. Their encouragement will be valuable in the journey ahead.

Worksheet 13.19

> **Who could be a good fit as an accountability partner? How could this person help you move toward achieving your ideal life vision?**

This is a big step for some people, so take your time getting used to the idea of sharing yourself in this way. While not absolutely necessary, having an accountability partner can be a game changer in helping you carve out the time and find the inner motivation to make your vision reality.

So, what comes up for you after reading this last stage of creating your ideal life? What will you do to keep yourself accountable and to help move yourself toward your ideal life?

Worksheet 13.20

> *What can you put in place to ensure the work you have done to look at where you are, where you want to go, how you will get there and how you will stay on track, will move from just thinking about this to making it happen?*

How important is this ideal life to you? Jot that down and refer back to it often. Perhaps this will make the difference on the days you need a bit of extra motivation.

As you start making progress creating your ideal life, how will you remember to be grateful for the progress you make, and the people who help you?

What can you do to embrace patience in your life?

> **And how will you keep yourself accountable? What can you do to stack the odds in your favor?**

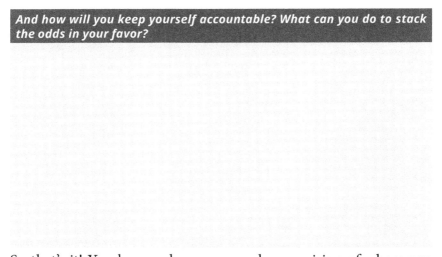

So that's it! You know where you are, have a vision of where you want to go, a plan to start you out, and some ways to help keep you on track. The rest is up to you. It is time for you to take those first few steps beyond this plan. It is time for you to create your ideal life!

I am excited for your journey ahead. Good luck and safe journey my fellow traveler!

If you own a business, are thinking of starting one, or are looking to make improvements in one you are involved with the next chapter will show you how to use the same process to move toward an ideal business!

Bonus: Real progress takes time and effort, and I have found developing a routine helps many of the people I work with—including myself! On the next page is an example of a few questions/habits you could use from different stages of the step back process. Feel free to use them, or create your own habits, that will help you develop a growth-oriented routine that is right for your own journey!

THE ART AND SCIENCE OF CREATING YOUR IDEAL LIFE

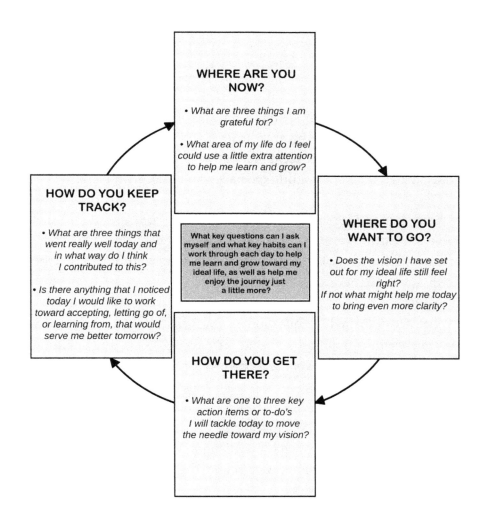

CHAPTER 14

Your Ideal Business

You're envisioning your ideal life, but you might also be wondering about your business if you are a business owner. Perhaps you think, "I see the vision for my ideal life, but what about my business? It's like a ball and chain holding me back from making it a reality!"

I know before I left my business, I faced this same question. I was able to exit the company, and it was the right decision at that time in my life. However I'm not saying that leaving your business is the only way to achieve your ideal life.

What if you turned the question around? Instead of asking, "Why is this business holding me back?" try asking "How am I holding my business back from being its own best self and allowing it to let me live my ideal life?"

As I mentioned earlier, my insecurities and lack of identity outside of the business were my biggest challenges. Without a well-rounded sense of identity, it was almost impossible for me to know how I was holding my business back.

Since stepping back I am now armed with my ideal life vision in the new business I am creating, I look at things much differently. Your life and business are connected and need to work together.

Today I am better positioned to create a business that works for me rather than the other way around. This well-rounded sense of purpose propels me to do whatever I can to make the business successful while dedicating time to other important areas of my life.

Now, let's have a look at what you can do to create or transform your current business into one that will help you achieve the life you want. Go through this chapter with your ideal life vision in mind, keeping your notes handy. This can help you see your business through a new perspective, one that can be instrumental in helping ensure your business vision aligns more wholly with your ideal life vision.

I want to reassure you that I know how much time and effort needs to go into a business, especially upfront. This process is not so much about keeping everything perfectly balanced between your work and your life. It's more about balancing what is important to you, including your business, so all the parts of your whole life are more harmonious.

> "If you aim at nothing, you will hit it every time."
>
> ZIG ZIGLAR, author, salesman, motivational speaker

What I propose is not your typical strategic plan. It isn't something you do once and put on the shelf. Instead, this is a strategic planning process that encourages you to step back regularly to check in with your vision and ensure you continue to take action to move forward, learn, and grow.

The process described in this chapter does lack some key elements that would round out the work into a complete strategic plan, but it is still a very powerful start.

What are the benefits of a strategic planning process? They include:

- Increased clarity about your company's present and future
- Better internal communication
- Improved accountability and project execution
- Greater sense of commitment and engagement from others
- Increased value of your business
- Decreased dependence on the business owner
- Improved quality of life for all

Most business owners can achieve all these things if they invest the necessary time and ask for help where they need it. Does this sound like something worthwhile?

If so, let's return to the step back process and its key elements, including the following questions:

Where are you now?

Where do you want to go?

How will you get there?

How will you keep yourself on track?

Many of the concepts are very similar for both your life and your business. I'll note any differences or additions and will also provide space so you can use this as a workbook.

I encourage you to do the work because I know how happy you will be a few months down the road when you see all the progress you've made.

STAGE 1: WHERE ARE YOU NOW?

In this stage, we will use our main questions that we used in the ideal life section as a start, then, we will do a SWOT analysis. A SWOT analysis is a strategic planning technique to help you assess your company's strengths, weaknesses, opportunities and threats. It helps you look at your company from a 360-degree perspective.

To help you stay accountable to the plan you have made, it's important to step back for a moment and ask yourself how important it is to you to have your ideal business. The following questions are here to help you accomplish this as well as help you with your journey ahead as you work through your plan.

As with the previous chapter I have included my own journey through these questions as a reference for yourself, based on the business I am currently building. There is no right or wrong way to answer the questions in this chapter. Be honest and do what feels most beneficial.

NUMB?

Worksheet 14.1

How is your mindset? Do a quick check in to ensure you still have a growth mindset in terms of the business. If not, what can you do to develop more of a growth mindset for creating your ideal business?

My answer:

I have a growth mindset. To ensure I keep it, I will commit to regular check-ins with my coaches and people who understand the entrepreneurial journey!

Your answer:

> **Can you describe, as objectively as possible, the situation your business is in and how you want to change it? What are the facts a reporter would observe?**

My answer:

> *The business has been steadily growing. I find myself doing more and more one-on-one coaching and having less time to build it. I have developed a couple of online courses that go along with this book and still have one more to build before I launch them all. I am enjoying all the work I am doing and want to ensure I can scale the business.*

Your answer:

> **What are you telling yourself about the state of your business? How is it affecting your journey toward your ideal life?**

My answer:

> *I am concerned if I keep going down the path of doing one-on-one coaching, eventually I will get so busy I will start neglecting the other aspects of my life that are important to me. I do not want this to happen again. How do I build a business that can deliver excellent service to clients and at the same time rely less on myself so I can live my ideal life.*

Your answer:

> *Do you believe everything you are telling yourself? Do the facts of the story match what you are saying? If you were talking to a true friend in the same situation, how would you speak to them? What advice might you offer? What might be more beneficial to tell yourself?*

My answer:

> *I fully believe that being armed with my life vision and connected to what matters to me will allow me to stay grounded and if I stay grounded I will be able to strategically run and grow my business in a way that fits my life. Follow your process, Dave. Figure out the next steps, be patient and move forward. You can have it all. All that is truly important to you. People believe in what you are doing, and they are willing to help you make it all a reality!*

Your answer:

> **What do you want to change internally, embrace, or release, so you can take the next steps in creating your ideal business?**

My answer:

> *You have people who can help you, Dave. You can trust them, and by doing that, they will help you build the business! You can let go of having to do everything and know everything. Trust others!*

Your answer:

What did you notice as you answered these questions? With bigger businesses, it can be a bit more complex to explain your situation, but by following this format and uncovering the deeper shifts you need to make, real progress can be made!

Now for the SWOT analysis.

In a SWOT, you take the time to step back and analyze your business from four perspectives. What are our company's strengths? What are its weaknesses? What are the opportunities? What are the threats? I will not provide too much more in terms of background on this as there is a lot of information on it readily available.

I have provided a quick example from my own business in each of the segments that follow.

Please step back for a moment to jot down the thoughts that come to you as you do the exercise. If you have employees, step back as a group and go through it together, if you can. If you listen to what they say and incorporate their thoughts, you may start to find that the business is less dependent on you.

Once you've done this analysis, you can revisit the previous key questions or just step back and see what insights you've gained.

Optional step: If you have time to go deeper and to gain more clarity on what drives value in your business, I would encourage you to take a peek at the Value Driver Worksheet in the next chapter before doing the SWOT analysis. It can provide extra insight into your business and the different elements that come together to create its value. If your eventual goal is to sell your business and reap the rewards of a sale, a better understanding of your value drivers is crucial.

NUMB?

Worksheet 14.2

STRENGTHS: *What is our company good at and what should we keep focusing on?*

One example from my business: *Passion to help others*

Your answer:

OPPORTUNITIES: *What can we focus on to create a competitive advantage? Often strengths will come to mind, which is great, but don't discount weaknesses or even threats. Sometimes they offer hidden opportunities.*

One example from my business: *Tap into the step back process and offer it as an easy to use online course that allows people an affordable option, and allows me to scale the business.*

Your answer:

WEAKNESSES: *What are we not good at that we either need to improve, outsource, release, etc.?*

One example from my business: *Marketing and product development*

Your answer:

THREATS: *What threats exist for our business both inside and outside the company? Anything from your overall well-being and the well-being of others, to the political environment are good to consider.*

One example from my business: *A key threat is the threat of not scaling business and having my work life interfere with my other key life aspects.*

Your answer:

Congratulations! You're now in that beautiful space of noticing, bringing awareness to where you are now, what you might need or want to shift into or out of. This, in and of itself, is very powerful. New ideas about the changes you will need (or want) to create a new future arise from here.

STAGE 2: YOUR DESTINATION – WHERE DO YOU WANT TO GO?

Now that you have a better idea of where you are, it's time to turn your sights to the future!

Turning your sights to the future is where you envision what you want for your business. This is your time to dream. As you work on this section, regularly refer back to your ideal life vision to make sure they support each other.

Once again, take some time for yourself, and follow along as I help you find more purpose and clarity with your business.

Try this exercise:

> *Find a quiet place.*
>
> *Get still, take a few deep inhales in and exhales out, and let your mind relax.*
>
> *Now, imagine a time in the future when your business is at its ideal state. Fully sink into the experience as though you are really there.*
>
> *Imagine walking around your ideal business.*
>
> *What do you notice as you talk to some of the employees?*
>
> *What are they saying?*

What are your customers telling you?

How about your suppliers? What are they saying?

Now turn your attention to yourself. How do you feel walking around your ideal business?

Stay lost in that feeling of having your ideal business for as long as you want before coming back to here and now.

Worksheet 14.3

What is coming up for you? What are you starting to notice could be in your ideal business?

• **BONUS** •

For a guided ideal business visualization please visit
www.davesinclair.ca/numbbustingresources
for a complementary download.

Next, establish your timeline.

Now that you've virtually experienced your ideal business, do you have a timeframe in mind for when it could be in place? If so, when?

Jot this date down so you have a target moving forward. There's no right or wrong answer, but many people find a goal of 2 to 5 years works well.

Worksheet 14.4

What is the target date for your ideal business to be in place?

As we did in an earlier exercise, think of your ideal business as a circle made up of different parts. What are the different areas of your business that need to come together and will make it successful?

Try to come up with about 6-10 segments. Here are some ideas to get you started, as well as an example of what my key business aspects are right now.

- Sales
- Legal and regulatory
- Brand/Reputation
- Marketing
- Accounting
- Operations
- HR
- Customer satisfaction
- Employee satisfaction
- Suppliers
- Strategic plan

YOUR IDEAL BUSINESS

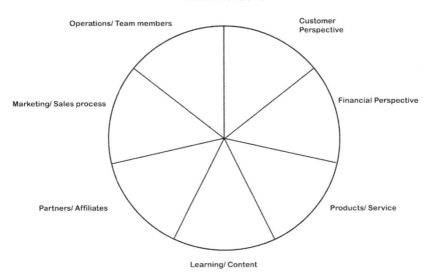

Now write down 6-10 key parts of your business, using words that make sense for you:

Worksheet 14.5

THE KEY ASPECTS OF YOUR IDEAL BUSINESS		

Now that you know your business aspects, divide the circle on the next page into equal segments, with one for each area. Then write one of your aspects in each piece of the pie. As in the ideal life exercise, the next step in the process will be to bring these different aspects to life by adding a mini vision for each one.

Worksheet 14.6

YOUR IDEAL BUSINESS VISION

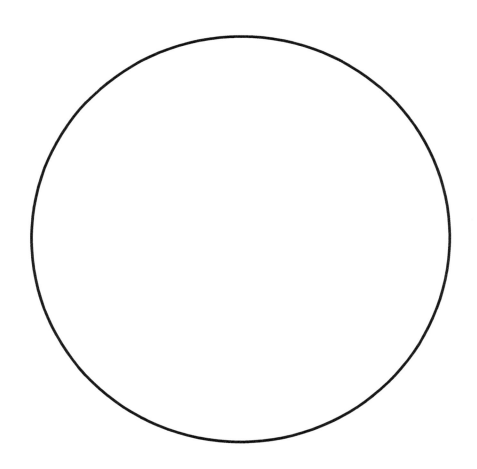

In the following chart, you're going to add two things about each aspect of your business:

- **WHAT** do you want this aspect to be like?

- **WHY** does it matter? In other words, how does it reflect what you value and how does it help your company, as well as everyone involved? This includes your employees, customers, suppliers, partners, and yourself.

Once you finish the chart, take time to come up with a shortened version of the what and why for your vision wheel, as we did in the previous chapter. This shortened version is like a mini vision. It describes how you see each aspect in its ideal state and gives you something to aim for. Use worksheet 14.8 to create this mini vision and then add it to the appropriate section of your vision on worksheet 14.6.

Doing this and adding it to your business vision will allow you to better track your progress toward your goals in these different areas. It will also help you inform others of what you are trying to achieve so they can help, as well as help you figure out which projects to undertake (or not). This vision is your compass guiding you forward.

Worksheet 14.7

BUSINESS ASPECT	WHAT YOU WANT	WHY IT MATTERS
My example: Products/Services	Our products and services are designed to be simple and intuitive. They range from a complementary worksheet to in-depth, one-on-one guidance.	Everyone who wants to embark on the journey of discovery and action can find a way that fits for them, and by leveraging technology I can offer my services in a way that fits my clients, helps me scale my business, and ensures I can keep up with my ideal life plans!

YOUR IDEAL BUSINESS

Worksheet 14.8

BUSINESS ASPECT	MINI VISION FOR THIS ASPECT (WHAT DO YOU WANT THIS TO BE LIKE AND WHY?)

YOUR IDEAL BUSINESS

Here is a current vision for my business for your reference. It's always a draft, and as I learn and grow or the market conditions change, I can modify it as needed. Revisiting it is important and your industry will dictate how often you may need to do that.

Are you gaining clarity about the values of your ideal business? (Your values will likely come from the chart where you said why these areas matter to you). They matter to you because they reflect the things you value.

How would you describe those values in a few words? If you were giving advice to a close family member who was thinking of starting a business, what would you say?

In the worksheet below first jot down your advice in the second column. Once you have done this, take a step back and ask yourself: What value or values, that is/are true to me, does this advice represent? Add this value word/phrase to the value column. You have likely just touched upon a key value, and a definition on how to bring it to life in your business! How might this help you and the business moving forward?"

Worksheet 14.9

VALUE WORD	WHAT ADVICE WOULD YOU GIVE SOMEONE LOOKING TO START A NEW BUSINESS IN TERMS OF ITS VALUES?

Do your chosen business values align with those of your ideal life?

This is important, because the more aligned they are, the more fulfilled you'll be in both your professional and personal life.

Your business values should guide your decisions and behaviors around every aspect of the company. Why? Because they influence your **brand**, your **reputation**, and your **success**. The more you can live and model the values of your business the more your employees will do the same. It's where you 'walk the talk'.

Keep your values in mind as you move forward because your values are the most trustworthy guides you can have, whether in business or in life. As a matter of fact, the closer you hold your values to your heart, the more you will embody them and the more aligned your actions will become to them.

Also, the more you give voice to your vision and values, inside and outside your business, the more powerful it all becomes. If you decide to do in-depth strategic planning—work with others in the company to create a shared vision and developing a process to ensure you make time to regularly move toward it—this can create some **real magic.**

STAGE 3: GETTING THERE

How are you doing in terms of where you are right now compared to where you want to go?

Divide the circle on the next page into how many business aspects you have, and then write the name of your key aspects into the different segments.

YOUR IDEAL BUSINESS

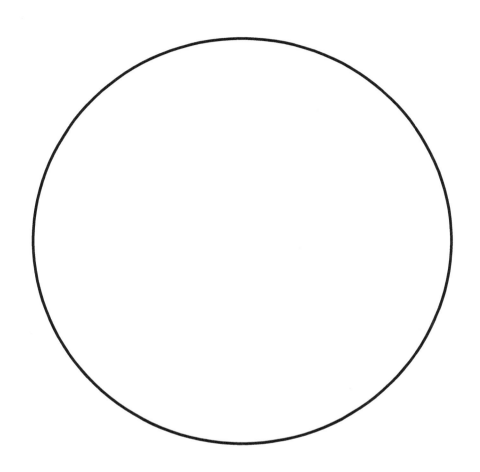

If there's a category where you're really knocking it out of the park, color in that complete segment, from the center to its outer edge.

If you're only halfway there, color it in halfway from the center, out.

If you're barely making a dent in that category, just color a little bit from the center, out.

I've included my own business pie chart as an example.

Worksheet 14.10

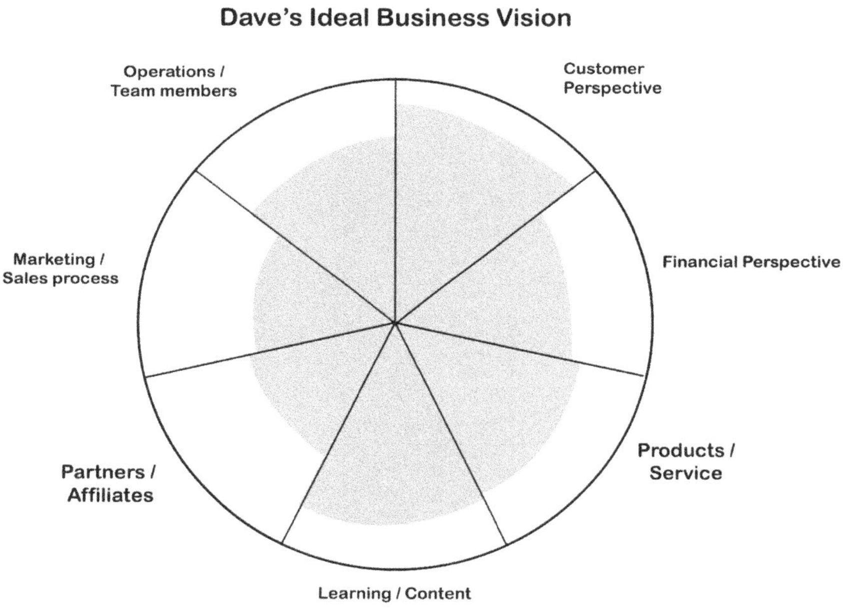
Dave's Ideal Business Vision
Operations / Team members
Customer Perspective
Financial Perspective
Marketing / Sales process
Products / Service
Partners / Affiliates
Learning / Content

When you're done, take some time to absorb what your pie is telling you. Think about how it feels to see your current reality in the context of where you want to go.

My pie chart tells me I am happy overall with the progress in my business so far. I have set good goals, and have the products and services I need to achieve my overall vision. I can also see that to get where I want to be financially, I will need to scale up the business. If I want to do that effectively, my best bet will be to do it in ways that don't require me to be directly involved.

Worksheet 14.11

> **Step back to examine your pie chart. What story does it tell? Which one or two aspects, if they were improved, would have the biggest impact on the business and help you to get your story going in the right direction?**

Next, decide what **one aspect** you could focus on that would have the **most impact** on your business. For me, the aspect that most stood out was marketing and sales. Take your time and go with what feels right to you.

> **What is the one aspect that you feel you want to work on first?**

Looking at what you've done so far, what are a few initiatives (a business improvement project) you could work on to move toward your ideal business vision within the first three months.

As a best practice, less is more. I suggest you focus on one initiative if you can, do it well, and then move to the next initiative.

In the context of strategic planning for a larger company, you may map out initiatives and action steps for more than one business area. Make sure that priorities are clear and that as many people as possible in your company have a role to play so they can help you achieve your vision.

Take a minute and jot down some possible initiatives and then circle the one you think will have the biggest impact on your business. Just let you mind run free and know that you do not have to do them all right now. You can always come back to this list in the future once you get your first initiative underway!

Some potential initiatives for me in marketing and sales include: Creating a marketing and sales plan for my ideal life online course, creating some new online courses, updating my website to reflect online courses available, creating a social media posting plan, etc.

A slight difference between an initiative for your ideal life or for your ideal business is around team members. If you employ others, think of who will be able to help you complete this initiative, and what deeper benefit is provided by bringing them into an initiative.

If it's only you, look at tasks you can outsource when it makes sense, especially as you get busier. Outsourcing doesn't have to be expensive. Instead, it can be quite informative to step back and check in to ask if doing certain tasks yourself makes the most sense, for you and the business.

How about you?

Worksheet 14.12

What are some potential initiatives that could improve a particular business area?

Choose one initiative that you feel will have the biggest impact on your business and also makes sense with your ideal life plan!

What is the first initiative that, when completed, will have the biggest impact overall on your business?

Next, fill out the chart on the next page with the one initiative you want to work on first, a few action steps you or someone in your business will take to accomplish it, and when it will be done. For me, it looks like creating a plan to market and sell the "My Ideal Life" course online.

Business Aspect: Marketing and Sales Process

Worksheet 14.13

Initiative: Market and sell "My Ideal Life" online course (as completed)	Why have you chosen this initiative? How will it help you reach your business (and even personal) vision? Doing this will allow me to serve people who would prefer to start out by doing an online course, as well as create a revenue stream that does not require me to trade hours for money.	
Team lead: Dave	Team members: Dave, Dennis, Amin	
Tasks (action steps to complete the initiative)	Who will do this?	When will this be done?
Finish beta testing online course	Beta testers	Oct 7
Meet with Amin to discuss marketing strategy	Dave/Amin	Oct 14
Create strategy for launch	Amin	Oct 21
Create landing page for course	Dennis	Oct 31
Soft launch and gather feedback/revisit plan for next steps	Dave/Amin/Dennis	Nov 30

Business Aspect This Initiative Will Help Improve:

Initiative:	Why have you chosen this initiative? How will it help you reach your business (and even personal) vision?	
Team lead:	Team members:	
Tasks (action steps to complete the initiative)	Who will do this?	When will this be done?

STAGE 4: STAYING ON TRACK

To help you stay accountable to the plan you have made, it's important to step back for a moment and ask yourself how important it is for you to have your ideal business.

For me, creating an ideal business is critical to supporting my ideal life. I have been on the other side of this, but now I strive to create a business that fits with, enhances, and fully supports my ideal life. Knowing this makes me want to persevere at doing the work I need to do to keep on track!

Worksheet 14.14

> *How about you? How important is this ideal business to you? Jot that down and refer back to it often. Perhaps this will make the difference on the days you need a bit of extra motivation.*

Follow the same process you used in previous chapters to answer the following questions in this stage. Review previous chapters, as needed.

> *As you start making progress creating your ideal business, how will you remember to be grateful for the progress you make, and the people who help you?*

What can you do to embrace patience in your business role?

> **And how will you keep yourself accountable? What can you do to stack the odds in your favor?**

Please note: If you are going to hire a coach to help you with your ideal life, business or transition, look for one with the life experience and the formal coaching credentials to help you best! There are many coaches out there with different skill sets and personalities. Find one who fits you and your situation.

Breaking things down into actionable steps will help you commit to moving forward. Once you've made significant progress with the first initiative, revisit the process and select the next one. And have fun as you start to see things happen!

TEAM ENGAGEMENT COUNTS

As I mentioned earlier, if you include your team in the process of strategic planning, the level of engagement that can result has some pretty significant benefits for your business.

Consider how the performance of the most engaged businesses compared to those with the least engagement, according to the Gallup Organization's "2017 State of the Global Workforce Survey":

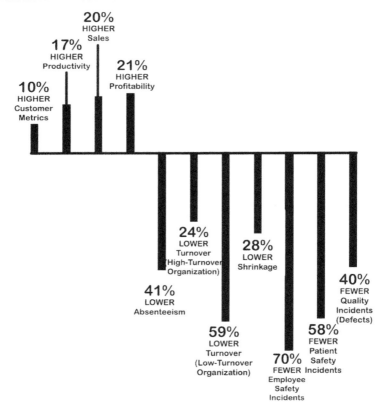

More sales, productivity and profitability?

Sure!

Less absenteeism, turnover, shrinkage, safety incidents and quality lags? **Absolutely!**

Great work! Throughout this chapter you have stepped backed to explore where your business is now, where you can take it, have laid out your first initiative that will kick start your journey, plus have a plan for staying on track. You have completed some significant work and I am hoping that you are starting to fill with optimism about where you and your business are headed. I wish you well as you take your first steps on the path ahead!

Next, let's see how all the work you've done culminates in the third and final step: your ideal transition!

CHAPTER 15
Your Ideal Transition

Transitioning out of a business can be very tough. There's a lot going on, and it isn't something most business owners deal with more than once in their life.

However, transitioning can be HUGELY beneficial for you, it can be a route toward creating and living your ideal life.

Remember how I left my business?

I had a lot of questions at the time, and perhaps you can relate to them:

- How much money is the business worth?
- How much money do I need upfront if I leave?
- How will I negotiate a buyout with my partners?
- What will I do if I leave the business?
- How will the business do without me?
- What will people say about me after I leave?
- What will my family think?
- What if I cannot find anything else to do?
- What does not working there mean to me?

With so many questions swirling around my head, it was a miracle I managed to leave at all! I was fortunate that I had a good idea around what the business was worth and what I would get paid. Still, agonizing over all those other questions was tough on me, my family, and the business itself. I found myself spending all my time ruminating, to the point I often sat frozen at my desk, feeling overwhelmed. I had too many questions and not enough answers. It left me feeling numb. Can you relate?

Well, if you can, you're not alone. The Canadian Federation of Independent Businesses found that 51 percent of owners have no plan on how they will transition out of their business and capture its value—value that they worked so hard to create.

The federation's 2012 report, "Passing on the Business to the Next Generation," also found:

- 80% of owners' overall wealth is tied up in their business
- 9% of owners have a formal written transition plan
- 38% of owners plan on exiting in 1-5 years
- 29% of owners plan on exiting in 6-10 years
- 85% are leaving for retirement reasons

I've read other reports with similar findings, and it still boggles my mind that only 9% of owners have a formal written transition plan and so, the message is very clear: Very few people do the necessary planning work to ensure successful transitions. Yet most business owners need proceeds from the business to fund the next stage of their life, and they want that stage to be one they can enjoy! People devote so much of themselves, sacrificing family and leisure time to build a business and they have 80% of their overall wealth tied up in their business, and yet, they leave transitioning out of it to chance? Wow.

Ready to see the path to the most meaningful time of your life?

Here's the point in your process where you leverage your self-reflection and planning to build the possibilities for your life and business.

Having a vision for your life, that you deliberately take steps toward, brings the kind of fulfillment that infuses everything you do with more passion and meaning. The decisions you make in your business when you know what you want from your life will not only work better for you, but can also make life better for your employees and bring added value to your business. And when your time to transition to a new chapter of life arrives; you'll continue to reap the rich rewards you've created for yourself.

Sounds good, doesn't it?

The thing you've learned by now is that it can be far more than just a dream. Self-reflection leads to committing things to paper. Then to creating goals. Then acting on them and finally to repeatedly sharing them with someone else so you're accountable. The evidence for your chances of attaining your dreams is undeniable if you follow those simple steps.

When you're three to five years from leaving your business, you should work on finalizing the transition details. (Basically dotting the i's and crossing the t's.), but when do you think the best time to start thinking about transitioning out of your business is?

Ideally, you want to start thinking about your transition even before you get in business. Thinking about this ahead of time can play a crucial role in your decisions about how you structure, operate, and build your business. If you did not think of the transition at day one when do you think the second best time to think of it is? You got it. It is right now.

It's a great time to start thinking through what an ideal transition would look like, so that you and the business can be more prepared for it. Why is that important? Because a business that is well-positioned for a sale or transition to a new owner is likely a business where the owner does not have to be there every day. Basically, it's one where your ideal life is not too far out of reach and your ideal business is humming right along.

Why do business owners put this off? There are many reasons, but many people cite not having the time to plan for a transition and not knowing where to start. With all the demands on them, it's easy to understand. But leaving things to chance is like leaving money on the table. And what business owner do you know wants to do that?

It's not just about the money, either. Your life—now and in the future—can be richer in every way if you're willing to reflect on the deep questions only you can answer. They put you in a passion-generating place where taking steps to realize your goals isn't as hard as you might think.

> "A life which is empty of purpose until 65 will not suddenly become filled on retirement."
>
> DWIGHT L. MOODY, evangelist and publisher

As Moody says, waiting until you're 65 years old or retired to find your purpose doesn't guarantee you'll find it. Plus, what are you losing by not living each day now with a sense of purpose?

Start now by figuring out your ideal transition with our four key questions:

Where are you now?
Where do you want to go?
How will you get there?
How will you keep yourself on track?

Try to remember that the process is a kickstart, meant to help you dip your toe in the water and spur you on to take the next steps. Next steps can include talking with your existing advisors to create a more extensive plan, or seeking out specialists who can help you move forward.

By taking the time to go through this chapter and then sharing your thoughts with advisors, including accountants and lawyers, you can help get everyone rowing the boat in the same direction. Just think of the time, effort, and money you can save if they are all working toward the same core objectives.

STAGE 1: WHERE ARE YOU NOW?

Take a step back to check in with your current mindset, situation, and if your inner voice is helping you or not. Of course, when I went through my own transition in 2011, I didn't have a coach at first or these tools. So my answers I provide as examples are how I feel I may have answered them as I pondered my exit.

YOUR IDEAL TRANSITION

Worksheet 15.1

> **How is your mindset? Do a quick check-in to ensure you still have a growth mindset in terms of the transition. If not, what can you do to develop more of a growth mindset for creating your ideal business transition?**

My answer:

> *Growth mindset? What's that? I think I am a positive person and believe I am in control, but I am not sure if I have a growth mindset. I'm going to look further into this idea and watch some TED Talks on the subject to help me out.*

Your answer:

NUMB?

> *Can you describe, as objectively as possible, your situation and your reasons for a transition? What are the facts a reporter would observe?*

My answer:

> *My business partners have no formal succession plan in place. As a partner, I have asked them about exiting the business. They told me not to worry about it, saying, "The money will be there when you are ready to retire." Another partner was bought out last year, and I was involved with this. I know the price he received for his shares. I am considering leaving as I am unhappy with my life. I am 70 lbs overweight, stressed out, drinking a lot, and not spending as much time with my family as I would like. We go on vacations and buy great things, but as soon as I do this, I seem to be buying and spending more and more in an attempt to find some happiness. Even on vacation, I find myself thinking of work, and as soon as I am back, I find myself right back where I was. Unhappy and looking for something to change.*

Your answer:

YOUR IDEAL TRANSITION

What are you telling yourself about this situation?

My answer:

> *I'm sure I am going to have a heart attack ANY DAY. Maybe I am an alcoholic. I have a job that pays very well, and my share of the profits in this business is amazing. Is this all there is though? I feel completely stuck and don't think anyone can help me. I am alone and have no idea what I would do if I left here. I just can't get happy! This is all I am good at. It's hopeless.*

Your answer:

NUMB?

> *Do you believe everything you are telling yourself? Do the facts of the story match what you are saying? If you were talking to a true friend in the same situation, how would you speak to them? What advice might you offer? What might be more beneficial to tell yourself?*

My answer:

> *You can make a choice, you can find your answers, and you can do it all in a way that is professional and represents the best solution. I am sure there are specialists who help people in this situation. If you could find a few of the answers to your questions about succession, perhaps you'd be a little less stressed and make changes in other areas of your life. What can you do to find someone who can coach you through this?*

Your answer:

YOUR IDEAL TRANSITION

> **What do you want to change internally, embrace, or let go of so you can take the next steps in creating your ideal transition?**

My answer:

> *I think I need to embrace the idea that I could use some help with this change I want to make. I need to give up the idea that I need to do this all on my own. I can find someone to help me through this!*

Your answer:

It's time to turn our attention to some transition planning basics. In the chart that begins on the next page, look at the questions and write down your insights. Next, rank each one on a scale of 1-10 (1 being the lowest, 10 being the highest) in terms of how comfortable you feel with your level of preparedness in each aspect now.

Please don't feel overwhelmed. Instead, imagine a time in the future when you do have the answers to these questions. How will you feel then? The step back process you have already learned is here to support you toward awareness and clarity!

Transition Planning Basic Aspect Questionnaire

Worksheet 15.2

ASPECT	INITIAL INSIGHTS	RANK 1-10
When would you like to transition out of the business?		
How do you see yourself transitioning out of the business? Is it sudden or gradual?		
As an owner, what do you do on a daily basis? How much does the business rely on you?		
What does an ideal business transition look, and feel like to you?		
What does your ideal life look, and feel like after you leave the business? Have you taken the time to consider what you will do, or how you will feel, if the business does not need you anymore?		

How much money will you need from the company to live your ideal life after you transition out of the business? What savings do you have outside the business to fund this?		
What is your business worth? How do you know this? What would an outsider say your business is worth?		
Is there a value gap between what you need to fund your next stage, what you have saved outside the business, and what you can extract from the business in a transition?		
How well do you understand what creates value in your business? What would an outside investor value in the business? What is your plan to increase the value drivers in the business if you need to? (Please see the upcoming value drivers worksheet for this.)		

What would you like to see carried on in the business that is important to you if you were no longer there?		
Do you know what the options are in terms of whom you can transition the company to? (Family, key employees, professionally managed, third party sale, private equity group, wind down, etc.) What options do you feel may be good, and what is it about this option that may be beneficial?		
If internal succession is an option how prepared are your internal successors? Have you had conversations with them about this? Are you all on the same page?		
Do you have a plan that will ensure the business can carry on, even if you are not there for an extended period?		

Where are you in terms of tax planning for the business and your personal finances to ensure as much money as possible stays with you in any form of transition?		
Is your will current, and does your estate plan cover personal and business assets? Is it in alignment with any agreements that may exist within the business?		
In terms of continuity and succession, how are you and other key people in the business insured? If you have partners, what happens in the event one of you becomes disabled or dies?		
Do you know your options on how to sell your business to a third party (i.e. business broker, mergers and acquisitions firm, etc.) or complete the financing for internal transition?		

Now that you've gone through some of the basic transition planning questions, let's take a step back again to rank the value drivers in your company.

Note: This table can also be used with chapter 14 (when you are building your ideal business) if your eventual goal is to sell your business to fund the next stage of your life. The table will help bring about ideas as to what might need attention, and what might have the biggest impact.

Read through the questions starting on the next page and answer each question on a scale from 1 (needs a lot of work) to 10 (our company is the best in class on this and we can prove it) as seen through the eyes of an external investor.

For this exercise, use the perspective of a professional who was hired to help a potential investor decide if your business is a good investment or not. Imagine you have an all access pass for a totally transparent view of the business and you can see everything. All of it: the good, the not-so-good, and the needs-a-lot-of-work.

Although not an entirely objective process, the score you get by totaling up all your individual rankings can be an eye opener. A lower total score would mean that you are leaving a lot of money on the table compared to a higher score if you were looking to sell your business. A lower score would also mean your business might not be as attractive if it went to market at the price you may want for it.

Value Driver Worksheet

*Worksheet 15.3**

VALUE DRIVER	VALUE DRIVERS FOR THE BUSINESS AS AN INVESTMENT	RANK 1-10
Industry Rating	Where is the company in the context of its industry in terms of overall size, growth potential, and how complex it will be to work in?	
Company Rating	How long has this company been around? Do they have a strong brand and a good reputation?	
Product/Service Rating	How do these companies' products and services look? Are they profitable? Are they in demand? Are there any risks?	
Competition Rating	How many competitors are there? What is keeping other competitors out?	
Personnel Rating	What does this company's staff look like? Who are the key employees? What is the turnover rate?	
Systems Rating	What systems does this company have in place? If a key person leaves, what systems, procedures, and information exist to ensure the company can keep moving forward?	

* These questions have been provided with the permission of Tom Gledhill from his book *XITPRO SYSTEM: Positioning Small Business Owners for Breaking the Mold and Successfully Selling Their Business.*

Cash Flow Rating	What is the ability of this business to produce a reasonable ongoing cash flow?	
Company Growth Rating	What is the capacity of this business for profitable growth?	
Customer Base Rating	What does the customer base look like for this business in terms of diversity and satisfaction? How reliant are customers on the company?	
Customer Concentration	How reliant is this company on a few key customers? Ideally no more than 10% of the company's overall business is coming from one customer.	
Supplier Rating	What is the status of these companies' suppliers? Are they overly reliant on any one supplier? What kinds of contracts are in place?	
Financial Presentation Rating	How reliable, accurate and useful are these companies' financial records?	
Lease Rating	Does this company have a long term, solid and transferable lease in place?	
Scalability Rating	How easy would it be for this business to increase production without extensive capital investments?	

Recurring Revenues Rating	What is the potential that current or future revenues will be guaranteed?	
Bankability Rating	How easy would it be for this business to get financing to fund future growth?	
Intellectual Property Rating	Does this company have unique ways of operating or specialized knowledge that gives them a significant advantage? If they do, is it properly protected?	
Other value drivers	Are there any other specific aspects of this business that create unique value?	
	Total score (max score = 170, if you did not add any other value drivers)	

Great work! You just completed the first stage in the process. I am curious as to what has come up for you as you filled in the last two tables. Do you feel like you now have a better understanding of the dynamics involved in creating a transition plan for your business?

> *Now that you stepped back to answer the questions around where you are, have looked at the Transition Planning Basics Aspects Table, and the Value Driver Table, what insights do you notice around how prepared you and your business are for a transition?*

STAGE 2: YOUR DESTINATION

I now invite you to take a minute to envision your ideal transition.

Get comfortable, take a few deep breaths, and let your mind relax into the scenario below.

Imagine you are somewhere in the future. You have just transitioned your business to new owners. Now really sit with and sink into this experience.

How does it make you feel? What do you notice? Are you fulfilled? Satisfied? What happened leading up to and during the transition that has allowed you to feel this way?

What do you notice about your partners, suppliers, customers, and employees in their reactions to the transition?

Take enough time to really experience this vision of your ideal transition, and when you are ready, come back to the present.

> *What is coming up for you? What are you starting to notice could be in your ideal business transition?*

• BONUS: IDEAL BUSINESS TRANSITION VISUALIZATION •

For a free guided visualization exercise that can take you deeper into this experience and the process ahead download the "Ideal Business Transition Visualization" at
http://davesinclair.ca/numbbustingresources

Ask yourself: Do I have a timeframe in mind for when this could happen? If so, when?

It is not critical to know exactly when you want to transition out of the business. However, setting an approximate date will allow you to create some internal urgency so you start addressing what needs to be accomplished to ensure yours and the business's future success.

Worksheet 15.4

Ideal Transition Potential Date

Again, as in previous exercises, think of your ideal transition as a circle made up of different parts. What are the different ways you need to look at your transition to come up with a holistic view of what will make it successful? What are the areas that would have to be addressed in your ideal transition plan?

If it helps, refer back to the tables in stage 1 of this chapter. What are some of the key aspects that jump out to you that would help you establish an ideal transition plan?

Try to come up with around 6-10 things. Here are some ideas to help get you started:

- When do I want to sell or transition out of the business?
- Who may be the best new owner of the business?
- Will my family be involved?
- How much money will I need to get from it?
- How prepared is the business for sale?
- How will I improve some of the value drivers? (Hint: Do you

have a plan for your ideal business from chapter 14?)

- Will my employees be retained?
- What do I want to leave behind/continue as my legacy?
- What will I do in my life after the sale? (Hint: Do you have a plan for your ideal life?)
- What is important?

Next, write down 6-10 key aspects of your transition. There's no right or wrong here. I am often asked if there is a "certain way" transitions are set up. The short answer is no. Just focus on what's important to you in a transition phase, your needs and wants.

Worksheet 15.5

YOUR IDEAL BUSINESS TRANSITION ASPECTS		

Now that you know what is important to you in a transition, divide the circle into equal segments, one for each aspect of the process. Then write one aspect in each piece of the pie.

Worksheet 15.6

YOUR IDEAL BUSINESS TRANSITION VISION

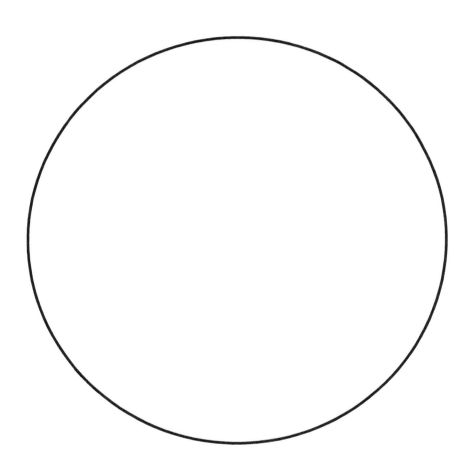

As before, the next step is to bring these aspects to life by describing:

- **WHAT** you want (how do you want this aspect to be in your ideal transition?)
- **WHY** it matters to you (how does it reflect what you value, and what is important about getting this right in your ideal transition?)

Use worksheet 15.7 to do this.

YOUR BUSINESS TRANSITION ASPECT MINI VISIONS

Once you have your whats and whys figured out, come up with a mini vision for each aspect that, when combined with the others, provides a well-rounded vision of your ideal transition. Use worksheet 15.8 to do this. Add this mini-vision to "Your Ideal Business Transition Vision" on worksheet 15.6.

NUMB?

Worksheet 15.7

TRANSITION ASPECT	WHAT YOU WANT	WHY IT MATTERS

YOUR IDEAL TRANSITION

Worksheet 15.8

BUSINESS TRANSITION ASPECT	MINI VISION FOR THIS ASPECT (WHAT DO YOU WANT THIS TO BE LIKE AND WHY?)

YOUR IDEAL TRANSITION

Having this vision is a powerful reminder for what your goals are, and a powerful tool to share with your key advisors, family, partners, or even employees. Sharing will help get everyone on the same page while pulling them in a common direction.

I didn't have this tool when I went through my transition. I wish I did! If I did, my vision might have looked something like what I have provided here. I provide it for your reference as you work on your business transition plan.

DAVE SINCLAIR IDEAL BUSINESS TRANSITION PLAN

- **My transition out** - Two years after I started this plan, I was able to leave the business on great terms with everyone, did not leave any messes behind, and can look back at my time here and smile
- **Money** - I have received enough money from the sale of my business to set myself up with a nice retirement nest egg, paid off my debts, have enough money to take a bit of time off, and start my new life!
- **Legacy of business** - The business is able to still be seen as one of the preeminent high end aftermarket industrial repair / machine shop business in Western Canada
- **Personal life** - I am able to create a life that allows me to be more fit, healthy, enjoy time with family and friends, find a few hobbies, find my next challenge, and be fullfilled.
- **New owners** - My partners have purchased my share of the business, and they are able to put things in place to ensure the future of the business is sound!
- **Continuity of business** - The business is able to carry on without me there and the people who work are able to still enjoy their work

Remember the 'value' work you did from the last two chapters? Take a look at it again. Once you are ready. I invite you to take a few moments to look at your transition through your personal and business values. What is important to you? How does the vision of your ideal transition align with your personal, and business values? Is there anything you might want to modify on your transition vision so it is more in line with these values? Does thinking of your transition give you deeper clarity into what your values truly are?

If you are feeling a bit overwhelmed that is OK. There is a lot here. Remember this doesn't have to all be done at once and you can return to this and modify it as needed. It is all a process and I find I am constantly deepening the understanding of my values, as well as further clarifying my vision of my life, business and transition. With small steps we move forward, learn, and grow into what it is we truly want.

STAGE 3: GETTING THERE

How are you doing in terms of where you are right now compared to where you want to go?

Divide the following circle into how many transition aspects you have, and then write the name of your key aspects into the different segments.

NUMB?

Worksheet 15.9

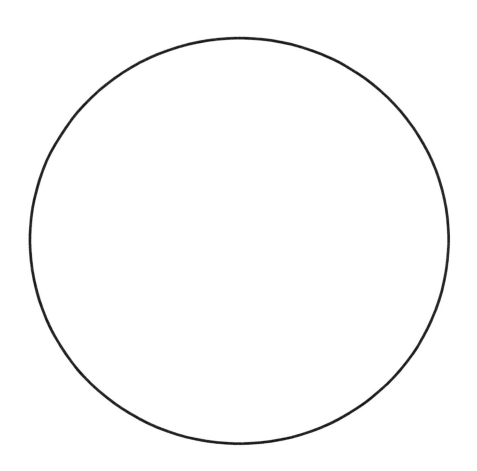

Next shade in each aspect in terms of how you think you are doing with 1 being, "This needs a lot of work," and 10 being, "I am solid with this aspect and have the plan and paperwork to back that up!"

Here is an example of how I think I would have ranked the different aspects of my transition, if I had done it.

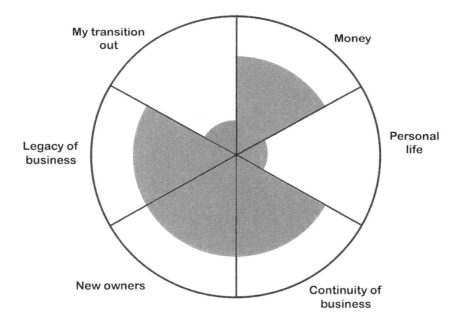

If there's a category where you are really knocking it out of the park, color in that complete segment, from the center to its outer edge.

If you're only halfway there, color it in halfway from the center, out.

If you're barely making a dent in that category, just color a little bit from the center, out.

When you are done, absorb what your pie is telling you. Think about how it feels to see your current reality in the context of where you want to go. What do you notice? What story is coming to life based on how you filled in the pie chart in the previous exercise, and what is this telling you about how prepared you are to transition out of the business.

For me, it was clear. When I colored in my pie chart, I had a pretty good idea what my shares were worth and that the business could carry on successfully without me being there, but I had no idea how to get my personal life going in the direction I wanted it to go in while I was involved in the business. I didn't understand how I could smoothly transition out. I felt stuck and had no idea how to tackle it all myself.

Now, take a look at your pie chart.

YOUR IDEAL TRANSITION

Worksheet 15.10

What is your transition pie chart telling you about what may need to be worked on, what is important to you, etc.?

Next, decide which one aspect you could focus on that would have the most impact on your business. Take your time and go with what feels right.

> **What is the one aspect you feel needs the most attention right now and will help you move your transition vision forward?**

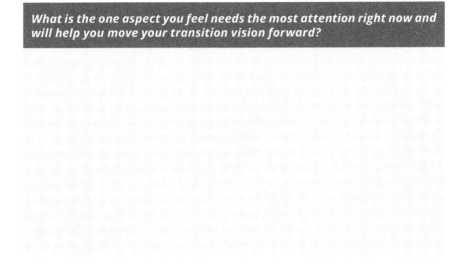

For me, the one aspect that would have made the most sense to tackle first was around my transition out of the business. This is something with which I had no real experience, so it makes sense why I was so anxious about it.

Looking at what you've done so far, what are a few initiatives (a project that you could complete in 3 months or so) in your selected aspects that you could work on to move toward your ideal business transition?

Write down some possible initiatives and then circle the one or two you think will have the biggest impact on your business transition plan. As a best practice, less is more. I suggest you focus on one initiative if you can, do it well, and then move to the next initiative.

My list could have included initiatives such as: find someone to help me figure out my transition plan, find seminars on transition planning and attend, take courses on transition planning, etc.

What are some potential initiatives that you could tackle that could improve your selected business transition aspect?

Next, select the one initiative that, if you were to complete it, would have the biggest impact in improving your overall comfort and state of preparedness for your business transition.

> **What is your first initiative that when completed will have the biggest impact overall on your business transition?**

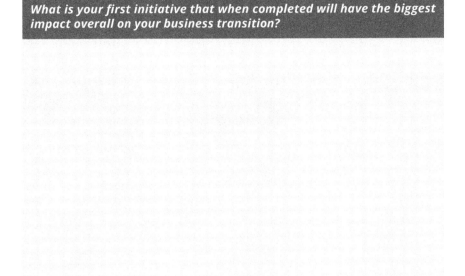

Go ahead and fill out the following chart with your first initiative, a few action steps you or someone in your business will take to accomplish it, and when it will be done.

As an example, I wrote this initiative assuming that I found a transition planning coach and had a few initial meetings with them. You may also note that the initiative still has the next steps TBD. I did this on purpose so you could see you don't have to have all the steps figured out. The key to a lot of the work you will be doing comes back to patience. Start the process, see what comes up, and then be OK with where you need to go. As you figure out more steps, add them to the initiative to help keep yourself accountable.

Initiative Figure out the steps to a smooth transition!	Why have you chosen this initiative? It is important to me that I leave the business on good terms, and that I have a plan with the steps I need to take to move forward. This will reduce my stress and improve my overall well-being as I go through this significant change.	
Team lead: Dave	Team members: Dave, perhaps a transition coach?	
Tasks (action steps to complete the initiative)	Who will do this?	When will this be done?
Research to see if I can find a coach that could help me with this. **Completed**	Dave	Nov 7
Interview and hire transition planning coach. **Completed**	Dave	Nov 21
Meet with coach and set next steps in the initiative. **Completed**	Dave, coach	Nov 28
Take some time to further define what a smooth transition looks like for me and the business.	Dave	Dec 7
Discuss valuation of business with CFO. What would my shares be worth?	Dave, CFO	Dec 7
Meet with a transition coach to discuss next steps.	Dave, coach	Dec 10

Now, it's your turn. Breaking things down into smaller, actionable steps helps make things more manageable, and writing it all down can increase your internal accountability. Once you have the first initiative well underway, it's time to revisit the process and select the next one. Enjoy the feeling of accomplishment!

NUMB?

Initiative	Why have you chosen this initiative? How will it help you reach your business transition (and even personal/business) vision?
Team lead:	**Team members:**

Tasks (action steps to complete the initiative)	Who will do this?	When will this be done?

STAGE 4: STAYING ON TRACK

To help you stay accountable to the plan you have made, it's important to step back for a moment and ask yourself how important it is for you to have your ideal business transition. The following questions are here to help you do this as well as help you with your journey ahead as you work through your plan!

For me, it was very important. Being able to transition out of the business and move on to a new life felt like a breath of fresh air.

> *After reading this chapter (and doing the exercises if you did) how important does working toward your ideal business transition feel to you? How can it impact you and others in positive ways?*

Continue with the following questions:

> *As you progress with your ideal business transition, both in the planning and execution phases, how will you remain grateful for your progress and the people who are helping you?*

YOUR IDEAL TRANSITION

What can you do to embrace patience in the process?

NUMB?

> **How will you keep yourself accountable? What can you do to stack the odds in your favor?**

Regardless of how you reach the milestone of a business transition, I am certain that you will want it to be smooth, profitable and fulfilling. I am hoping that the exercises that I provide in this book have aided in moving you toward this.

You may notice that whether you are creating your ideal life, business or transition, there is little difference in how I see approaching them. Moving forward I invite you to tap into the 4 key questions in the step back process; where are you now; where do you want to go; how will you get there, and how will you keep on track. I invite you to see how you might apply them to different situations, transitions or changes on your journey. As we close the second portion of this book my challenge to you is this: What can you do to step back just a bit more often as you move through life? How can pressing pause and stepping back become an ally for you?

CHAPTER 16

A Call to Action

Transitions don't happen overnight. Ideal businesses and lives are "ideal" because there is striving involved. So, please, don't be hard on yourself if you don't feel you've gotten anywhere fast in working toward your ideal life, business, or transition goals right after reading *Numb?*

One thing I hope you have gained after reading *Numb?* is that you have become more in touch with what calls out to you from within. This calling is what will make your journey richer and more meaningful. The next step is to use *Numb?* as a resource to start your journey. It is meant to be something you can continue to use at your own pace, as a workbook and a process.

It takes stepping back from all that keeps you feeling numb about your business and life to plan and grow new habits, Ultimately, it comes down to this: What is it that you really want out of life? What is important to you, and how do you end up at the finish line having lived a life full of your own unique meaning and purpose?

Once you answer these questions for yourself, things can start to change. And change for the better.

For me, the overall process we go through here has become a way of life. By gaining insight and clarity about myself and by repeatedly

A CALL TO ACTION

PAUSING and STEPPING BACK, the process gets easier, and now I get to work with and watch others benefit from PAUSING and STEPPING BACK.

If you want to, you can create change, improve your life and business, and bring more of the real YOU into all of your experiences. Just keep asking yourself questions like; Where am I now? Where do I want to go? How will I get there? How will I keep myself on track? The process can be applied to any transition, change, or improvement you may face.

When you reflect on the issues that rise up for you and come up with answers that touch what matters to you, the results are incredible. Just relax, take some quiet time for yourself with *Numb?* and have fun with it. Feel free to use what works, leave behind what does not, and for you own use, modify things to fit your style, and needs.

If you want help to move aspects of your life, business or business transition forward, I recommend working with a certified coach such as myself. As a kick start you can also enroll in my online course, "Create a Road-Map to Your Ideal Life" at www.davesinclair.ca. In this course you can build on the lessons introduced in *Numb?* taking you even further on your journey to your ideal life!

Please check back often as I add more courses and resources. I plan on adding a self-paced course for "Your Ideal Business," and "Your Ideal Transition" soon!

I hope you understand that you are not alone and others are working through similar questions in efforts to transform their lives too.

I'm an idealist who figured out how my ideal could become my day-to-day reality. Your ideal can be your reality, too.

I wish you all the best in the fulfillment of your ideal everything!

Dave Sinclair

❦

Please connect with me on my website at www.davesinclair.ca and let me support you on your journey. I'm a certified coach, and my specialty is helping business owners live a fulfilling life while growing their businesses.

To take the next stage in your journey, please visit www.davesinclair.ca/services to sign up for the "My Ideal Life" online course, and other courses as they become available. All courses include workbooks, videos, and guided visualization exercises as well as other resources to help you take your next steps.

If you'd like to inquire about one-on-one coaching, ask a question or share how this book helped you, email me at dave@davesinclair.ca. I look forward to hearing from you.

APPENDIX
Further Reading

Please visit **https://www.davesinclair.ca/numbbustingresources** for a link to my partial reading list. It includes an up-to-date list of useful books and mini book reviews.

Acknowledgements

What a journey! Over the last 49 years of my life – especially the last 10 – there are so many people, and experiences that have in some way or another influenced me and led to the book you are reading.

First and foremost, for my ever supportive and loving wife Gaylene. You, through all the good times and the challenges, have provided me with the motivation to be better. You have always been open and patient with me. I love you with all my heart and am so excited to continue our journey together. I am forever grateful.

For my sons Jordan and Jacob. I love you both unconditionally and only want the best for your own personal journeys. You are both amazing men and I am so excited to watch your paths unfold. Be true to yourselves and live your own personal definitions of success. I am here whenever you need, and for you my sons, I am forever grateful.

For my Mom and Dad. You have always been there for me and I am so grateful for our life on the farm. This provided much insight into life and work in general. In fact, it was not till much later in life that I realized just how much I missed more open spaces that led Gaylene and I back to the acreage we now find ourselves fully settled on. Thank you so much for all you have provided and taught. I am forever grateful.

For Ron and Nancy. Thanks for raising such a wonderful daughter and for accepting me into your family. You have been rocks for us all. Whether it was at the hockey rink helping out with the boys, teaching the kids to ski, or burning the garlic toast, you have always been a calm, caring, and steady influence on us all. I am forever grateful.

For the rest of my family. Thank you for being patient with me, accepting of me for who I am, and for being part of my overall picture of a life well-lived. I may not say it often enough but I love you all, and I am forever grateful to have you in my life.

For all my friends. I am thankful for you all. For friends, I am close with now, and for those, I was close with and have drifted away from, you have all touched my heart.

For my friend Peter. I am always thankful and indebted to you for your listening ear, and willingness to offer your perspective. I may not always listen, but I do always hear.

For my friend Pat. I am forever grateful for moments of wonder around lightning and thunder, and how this demonstrated to me how simple life can really be.

For all of my clients and people, I coach or consult with. I am grateful that you have put your trust in me. As I often tell you, your insights through our work are also a gift to me. I get so much out of our sessions as I watch you discover your own truth and path.

For all the great authors, teachers, mentors, and others I may not have referenced directly in the book. I thank you for all your wisdom. I am forever grateful for all of you and what you have contributed to the world, and my own personal development.

I would like to acknowledge a few special mentors and teachers I have had along the last 10 years.

Jack Beauregard. I would like to thank you for teaching me that business owners face much more than the technical challenges that a business transition brings. You taught me the importance of addressing the deeper side of the transition question that many business owners face. Who am I, if not the business owner? Your work lives in the pages of this book and has forever influenced me. I will be forever grateful for that.

Dr. David Drake. Although I do not know you personally, your influence has made an impact in my life, my coachees' lives, and also this book. I completed a certification in narrative coaching which was developed and taught by Dr. Drake. The approach of helping people create a more empowering narrative in their mind can be seen in certain spots in this book, and I would like to thank you for helping me deepen and further strengthen the process I work through with my clients. A good example of the influence narrative coaching has had on me can be seen in questions introduced in chapter 7. Narrative coaching consists in taking a step back to see what it is you may be telling yourself about the situation and then seeing if you can find a more empowering story to take place of your old narrative. Thank you Dr. Drake for deepening my understanding of the power of our internal narratives.

For the entire team that helped get the book to this point, I am grateful. Special thanks go out to Kathy Curtis who coached me in the early stages of writing this book, and to Lyda Mclallen who coached me across the finish line. I am forever grateful for your help, encouragement, and assistance.

I am certain I could go on forever with these acknowledgments, and for the sake of brevity, I will conclude by extending my gratitude to all I have met and worked with on my journey. For those of you I have not met, I want to offer an acknowledgment ahead of time, as I am certain you too will have more to contribute to this ever-evolving journey!

In love and gratitude,

Dave

CPSIA information can be obtained
at www.ICGtesting.com
Printed in the USA
BVHW080006231220
596003BV00007B/164